I may, I suppose, regard myself or pass for
being a relatively successful man. People
occasionally stare at me in the streets—
that's fame. I can fairly easily earn enough
to qualify for admission to the higher slopes
of the Internal Revenue—that's success.
Furnished with money and a little fame
even the elderly, if they care to, may
partake of trendy diversions—that's pleasure.
It might happen once in a while that something I said or wrote was sufficiently heeded
for me to persuade myself that it represented
a serious impact on our time—that's
fulfillment. Yet I say to you—and I beg you
to believe me—multiply these tiny triumphs
by a million, add them all together, and
they are nothing—less than nothing, a positive
impediment—measured against one draught
of that living water Christ offers to the
spiritually thirsty, irrespective of who
or what they are.

Malcolm Muggeridge

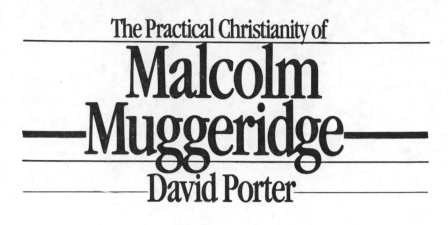

The Practical Christianity of
Malcolm Muggeridge
David Porter

Foreword by C. Stephen Board

INTER-VARSITY PRESS
DOWNERS GROVE
ILLINOIS 60515

Published in the United States of America by InterVarsity Press, Downers Grove, Illinois, with permission from Marshall Morgan & Scott, England.

InterVarsity Press is the book-publishing division of Inter-Varsity Christian Fellowship, a student movement active on campus at hundreds of universities, colleges and schools of nursing. For information about local and regional activities, write IVCF, 233 Langdon St., Madison, WI 53703.

ISBN 0-87784-971-4

Printed in the United States of America

Library of Congress Cataloging in Publication Data

Porter, David.
    The practical Christianity of Malcolm Muggeridge.

    1. *Muggeridge, Malcolm, 1903-*   I. *Title.*
BX4705.M767P67   1984   282'.092'4   83-26442
ISBN 0-87784-971-4

17   16   15   14   13   12   11   10   9   8   7   6   5   4   3   2   1
98   97   96   95   94   93   92   91   90   89   88   87   86   85   84

For Malcolm and Kitty

Now I saw in my Dream, that thus they sat
talking together until supper was ready. So when
they had made ready, they sat down . . . and all
their talk at the table, was about the Lord of the Hill.
John Bunyan, *Pilgrim's Progress*

Foreword

Malcolm Muggeridge, more than any other contemporary that comes to mind, has lived out the Old Testament book of Ecclesiastes. He knows the pursuits of life "under the sun," including the worlds of fame, politics, physical pleasures, wealth and intellectual achievement. He has seen the most hopeful (or at least most widely touted) attempts at human progress and happiness, and he has returned from all such experiments or claims with a message of "vanity, vanity" for the rest of the world. India, England, the Soviet Union, southern California, New York, London or Paris, all is vanity under the sun and a striving after the wind.

If C. S. Lewis embodies the twentieth-century quest for truth in the academic world, then by trial and error Muggeridge incarnates that quest in the world of the media, politics and public life. Lewis knew well "the best that had been thought and said in the world," to borrow Matthew Arnold's principle for what was needed for the "criticism of life." Muggeridge knows the best that has actually been done and promised. He has seen it as a correspondent in Moscow in the thirties or as a teacher in India earlier. As a journalist and television personality he has known life in the sun as well as under it. Earthly progress, finally, he came to see as "an ascent that ran downhill; plenty that turned into a wasteland; a cornucopia whose abundance made hungry; a death wish inexorably unfolding."

But like the world-weary author of Ecclesiastes, Muggeridge leaves his readers with numerous questions about his own world view, especially about his theology and his practice of the Christian life amid the wreckage

1

of dashed secular hopes. David Porter's book explores, one by one, the reconstructed philosophy out of which this modern English Christian lives his concluding years.

Among the typical questions we might ask are some like these: What is the chronology of Muggeridge's own pilgrimage toward Christ? How has he come to understand the key doctrines of Christianity and does he count them to be important? What is the place of the Bible in his Christian practice? Why has he been reluctant to identify with any existing church, at least until recent months? Why does he think petitionary prayer is a spiritual impertinence or unimportant? If God counts the hairs of our heads, he must attend to our laundry list of petitions!

To David Porter's credit, he poses some plausible counterarguments to Muggeridge's views in this volume, and that includes the chapter on prayer. But the reader will have to make up his own mind on each topic. I find it delightful to have a knowledgeable evangelical like Porter standing in for us to ask the kinds of questions we want asked. Especially is this valuable since Muggeridge does sense some distance between himself and the evangelicals (page 112).

That, in fact, brings us to the contribution this man's life has made in recent years. He bears the distinctive marks of a twentieth-century Christian. His credibility is his life and that life projects traits like the following.

Malcolm Muggeridge minimizes sectarian and denominational matters, what is commonly called "polemics," in the interest of the larger battle with the false gods of secular culture. On occasion he has come across as downright hostile to the clergy, the established churches and doctrines he deems irrelevant. "Institutional Christianity, it seems to me, is now in total disarray, and visibly decomposing, to the point that, short of a miracle, it can never be put together again with any semblance of order or credibility."

Allowing for a certain excess in language—what I would like to call Muggorrhea—will go a long way toward understanding this man's sometimes sweeping indifference to great doctrines. On one occasion in 1968, he dispatched the Trinity, the Immaculate Conception (his term) and the historicity of the Gospels as "perfectly comprehensible, perfectly harmless, and—as far as I am concerned—totally without significance. . . . I neither believe nor disbelieve them, and feel no inclination to defend or denounce them." We can assume he would not assemble his views that way in the 1980s, after his acceptance into the Roman Catholic Church.

Even those of us who believe Muggeridge does not have good taste in churches must grant that the very idea of "taste" in such matters betrays a uniquely twentieth-century style of being a Christian. His sense of cultural crisis and spiritual desperation understandably makes sectarian controversies moot and boring to all but the specialists. At the same time I wonder if those of us who are half his age can take the same position. We have families to raise and ministries we want to see flourish, preferably close to the biblical ideal. But you see my point—that Muggeridge's aloofness from ecclesiastical specifics marks him off as a modern Christian. It's the same with C. S. Lewis, Charles Colson and even Billy Graham.

A second characteristic of this twentieth-century Christian is his recognition that some root pathology is beneath several key social issues. Abortion, pornography, the welfare state and euthanasia are all expressions of moral and philosophical bankruptcy. Abortion implies self-centeredness; pornography discloses erotomania; the welfare state betrays a secular quest for the kingdom

3

of Man; and medical advances, for Muggeridge, sound
alarms of the coming tyranny of the majority over the
old, the helpless and the poor.

"I have seen pictures of huge, ungainly, prehistoric
monsters who developed such a weight of protective shell
that they sank under its burden and became extinct. Our
civilization likewise is sinking under the burden of its own
wealth, and the necessity to consume it; of its own security, and the ever more fabulously destructive nuclear
devices considered essential to it. As this fact sinks into
the collective consciousness, the resort to drugs, dreams,
fantasies and other escapist devices, particularly sex, becomes ever more marked."

For many Christians, the world is full of scornful
trends and practices, and they proceed to scorn them
without the complementary ability to link symptoms to
diseases. What could be an opportunity to change the
world, by properly interpreting it (to reverse Marx), is
thus lost, and the Christian "prophet" winds up a mere
scold. Muggeridge is rarely dismissed as a petty moralizer
because he has an interpretation of things that transcends mere moralizing. He is not a Pharisee, a prig or a
mere curser of darkness. Ultimately he bears witness to
the Light.

Probably for this reason, Muggeridge has a natural-
ness about his witness to Christ. On William Buckley's
television talk program, "Firing Line," the conversation
turned to the awkwardness of discussing religious ideas
among secularized people. Buckley observed that any
reference to God or Christ in a dinner conversation usually met with icy discomfort. Muggeridge could muster
no empathy at all for the problem. "I haven't found that
to be the case."

Most of us have found it a problem. And this leads to

what is probably Muggeridge's greatest gift as an ambassador for Christ in this century—his role as a communicator, whether in print or in person.

Here is what might be called a "testimony" by a master of English prose:

"I may, I suppose, regard myself or pass for being a relatively successful man. People occasionally stare at me in the streets—that's fame. I can fairly easily earn enough to qualify for admission to the higher slopes of the Internal Revenue—that's success. Furnished with money and a little fame even the elderly, if they care to, may partake of trendy diversions—that's pleasure. It might happen once in a while that something I said or wrote was sufficiently heeded for me to persuade myself that it represented a serious impact on our time—that's fulfillment. Yet I say to you—and I beg you to believe me—multiply these tiny triumphs by a million, add them all together, and they are nothing—less than nothing, a positive impediment—measured against one draught of that living water Christ offers to the spiritually thirsty, irrespective of who or what they are."

Students of rhetoric will recognize here the periodic construction in which suspense is built up through a chain of parallels until a climactic revelation is made. The apostle Paul's testimony in Philippians 3, as expressed in the King James Version, has a similar pace ("as touching the law, a Pharisee . . ."), and likewise resolves the tension in Christ ("what things were gain to me, those I counted loss for Christ . . .").

Despite a becoming modesty in Muggeridge's written and spoken language, he might be accused of what he himself found in G. K. Chesterton—"a certain ingrained flippancy in his whole attitude of mind." As an example, note his handling of polls, surveys and public opinion statistics.

"... I have long considered that the Romans were more sensible in using the entrails of a chicken rather than a slide rule to forecast the future.

"Perhaps the ideal thing would be to use Dr. Gallup's entrails, which would have the additional advantage that they could only be used once."

Now you know why Muggeridge is referred to as a curmudgeon. A younger writer could rarely get away with this sort of thing, and an older one had better have a lot more to say. This surely is what distinguishes this British curmudgeon from an American one of a few decades ago, H. L. Mencken. In Mencken the assault, the shock, the insult were all that he had to offer. He was an entertaining cynic. In Muggeridge, his shocks are comic relief, swift asides en route to cosmic relief. And I can't imagine a Muggerophile who would want to do without them. His wit is himself.

That finally is what so many people love about Malcolm Muggeridge. The gap between himself and his words has become almost imperceptible. In this his most explicitly Christian phase, he is saying what he thinks. Thus he serves his generation. When he is gone he will leave no school of thought or train of followers, no "method" to duplicate himself.

Indeed no evangelistic program could have yielded a character like him. No writing school or course would give us Mug prose. Television could probably not market a second Muggeridge, but our generation has desperately needed one of them.

God made him by hand.

C. Stephen Board
Carpentersville, Illinois

THE PRACTICAL CHRISTIANITY
OF MALCOLM MUGGERIDGE

Introduction: Encountering Malcolm Muggeridge

A man can't always be defending the truth; there must
be a time to feed on it.

C. S. Lewis

I

This book is about Malcolm Muggeridge, disciple of Christ.
It is not an analysis of his writings, nor a biography,
although in the writing of it I have often made use of the
studies and biographies that already exist. It is based very
largely on conversations with him, and it is concerned with
the practical, everyday experience of being a Christian as
Malcolm and Kitty Muggeridge experience it in their daily
lives. The question that the book explores is not 'Is Christianity true?' That is taken for granted, and Malcolm has
argued the case energetically elsewhere. The question I
have taken as my starting point is instead, 'What difference
does being a Christian make to the way one lives one's life;
and how does one obtain this faith for oneself?'

I first became aware of Malcolm Muggeridge in January

1968, when he resigned from the Rectorship of Edinburgh University. The authorities had disciplined the editor of the student magazine for an article advocating drugs; the student body, at the same time as protesting over the incident, demanded that the university health authorities should make contraceptives available to the students. In neither situation was Muggeridge prepared to support the students. Confrontation was inevitable, and in a rectorial address which attracted wide publicity, Muggeridge publicly resigned.

I had not long left school. As a family we were very late in acquiring a television, so I had not seen much of Muggeridge's prodigious media output. The only piece of his writing that stuck in my mind was his debunking of Claude Eatherly, a visionary lunatic who claimed to be living in mental turmoil because he had personally commanded the atomic raid on Hiroshima. John Wain, a poet of whom at the time I was inordinately fond, had written a long poem about him in which he blamed the rest of us for letting Major Eatherly do our dirty work for us. Like Mr. Wain, I fell for the Eatherly legend completely, and was not at all pleased to find Malcolm Muggeridge's gleeful review of a book by Bradford Huie, *The Hiroshima Pilot*. I thought Mr. Wain's poem much more inspiring than the bald facts presented by Muggeridge – notably the fact, discovered by Mr. Huie, that Eatherly had been nowhere near Hiroshima at the time of the raid.

Muggeridge was by then well established as a debunker, a sardonic bystander of the twentieth century who had been present at many of its most significant moments and had taken none of them very seriously. His anthology, *Tread softly for you tread upon my jokes*, had been published in 1966. One reviewer observed: 'The nervous tension produced in Mr. Muggeridge by his need to stay on the ladder while kicking it away is immensely bracing.' I had dipped into the book, and could see the point, but I wasn't willing to forgive Mr. Muggeridge too readily for losing me the Eatherly legend.

And then in January 1968 I turned on the radio and heard the Edinburgh sermon. I remember going out next day to look for a copy in a newspaper. For several weeks afterwards I rolled its phrases round in my head, sometimes walking home from work muttering under my breath in biting, Muggeridge tones, 'So, dear Edinburgh students, this is likely to be the last time I address you, and this is what I want to say – and I don't really care whether it means anything to you or not.' It was in the days before television impersonator Mike Yarwood cornered the market in 'doing Muggeridge', and I didn't know – having been deprived of the blessing of television for so long – that for a proper Muggeridge impersonation you had to hold your head on one side, smile broadly and tug your ear. But I loved his prose; it was like the poetry of Dylan Thomas; it cried out to be read aloud.

Although it was the language which first attracted me to Malcolm Muggeridge's writings, and in due course to his broadcasts, I was soon fascinated by what he was saying. I was a Christian, brought up in a Christian home. I was at college at the time and was involved in the college Christian Union, and I had also begun to get one or two things into print and was involved in poetry readings and other arts events in Merseyside and further afield. I was beginning to feel my way into the subject of how Christians should be trying to relate to the society in which they find themselves. Now here was somebody, deeply involved in the media, a famous writer, relating (if controversially) to students – and using the language of Christianity. His text for the Edinburgh sermon was 'Blest are the pure in heart'; its title, 'Another king'. In it he spoke directly and powerfully. 'As far as I am concerned, it is Christ or nothing'; on the Beatitudes – 'the most sublime words ever spoken'. I knew little of Muggeridge, but he certainly sounded like somebody who had put the scepticism of the past behind him. I accepted the assurances of many friends who had heard (usually from their friends) that Muggeridge had 'become a Christian'; and I was thankful, not only for his sake, but because the more Christian writers of that calibre the better by my reckoning.

But hard on the heels of the Edinburgh Sermon came *Jesus Rediscovered*, a phenomenally successful collection of his writings on Christianity which Muggeridge compiled reluctantly (he disliked the idea of an unretouched anthology) at his publisher's request. I bought a copy and read it. It left me rather perplexed. The Edinburgh sermon was there in its entirety; there were pieces which I found moving and helpful – some of them written several years before, which seemed to cast doubt on the theory that he had only recently become a Christian; and there were others which seemed to cast doubt on whether Malcolm Muggeridge was a Christian at all. In a piece entitled 'Am I Christian?', he simply said he didn't know. When he addressed the question 'Is there a God?', he called God 'something' – a usage which rang little alarm bells in my orthodox mind. I could see that some of these articles were dated several years before the book was published. But why had he allowed them to stand? Presumably because he still believed in them.

I was discovering for the first time what I have come to think of as the Muggeridge conundrum. I believe very strongly that the central truths of Christianity are capable of being expressed without qualification, in human words. Muggeridge, who has learned in his profession to be wary of words anyway because he knows what they can be used for, has said many times that words and definitions are often so limited that they are of little use. My instinctive reaction, to think of him as somebody whose religious beliefs put him at best on the fringes of biblical Christianity, was countered by two things; one was his increasingly prominent and courageous stand on issues with which Christians strongly identified (for example, his part in the founding of the Festival of Light); and the books which he was writing. A string of them following *Jesus Rediscovered* all dealt with Christian subjects or promoted a Christian perspective on some topical issue or other. Some of them became, and still are, books which I have found among the most challenging and helpful to me in my own Christian life; the two volumes of autobiography with their profoundly Christian view of current times; *Christ and the Media; Something Beautiful for God; Jesus, the Man who Lives*. I rapidly came to the conclusion that however oddly (from the point of view of accepted formulations) he might express himself, Muggeridge clearly had a vibrant, living faith, and one which, to judge from the sales of his books, had helped thousands of people all over the world.

Early in 1982 I wrote to Malcolm Muggeridge and asked if I could visit him to discuss my proposal for a book which would consider the practical aspects of his Christianity. He responded generously, and over twelve months I have had the opportunity of talking to him about his faith and his experience. My sources have been his published writings, his media pronouncements, and his conversation. It is not a book written out of a long acquaintance with him. Others are well placed to write such books, and have done so and will I hope do so again. This is the record of a personal encounter with Muggeridge, over a comparatively brief period. I put it to him that such a book might well be of great help to people who had observed his faith, responded to the power of books such as *Jesus the Man Who Lives*, and wanted to know how to have such a faith for themselves. This notion was immensely appealing to him, and much of our conversation was directed along those lines.

II

An indignant flurry of wings and a loud squawking met Malcolm as he closed the door of the run securely behind him and bent to fill up the feed tray. 'Now, ladies,' he remarked genially, 'you may shout as much as you like, and it will do you absolutely no good.' He stood back and scanned the ground. The hens, gently but firmly pushed aside in the search for eggs, screeched again. A few minutes later, grunting with satisfaction, Malcolm emerged from the poultry-run and displayed a basket with a dozen eggs.

Feeding the hens is a daily ritual in a life which is organised and predictable. The Muggeridges rarely go far from home; they follow the same daily routines, lunch on the same food almost unvaryingly, and walk the same well-loved walks at the same time most days. They like it that way. When in their company, one of the things that strike you is the delight they take in the endless variety they find in the familiar patterns.

They live in Park Cottage, a comfortable, roomy, slope-roofed home just outside Robertsbridge, in East Sussex. You get there by taking a steep road out of Robertsbridge and turning down a long straight lane, among oast-houses and green fields. It's easy to see why they do not bother to travel much these days, though Malcolm will drive to the station sometimes to collect visitors. It is an idyllic place, and full of associations for them. Near at hand is the large house they rented for several years ('Three pounds a week rent we paid. . .'), where their children grew up. When the children left home and the house was too large for them they simply moved across to Park Cottage.

A long refectory table dominates the kitchen. They do not eat extravagantly, but mealtimes are joyous occasions, with a good deal of laughter. Kitty makes yoghurt and bakes her own bread. Malcolm has appeared in a book featuring famous vegetarians, but they are tolerant on the subject and visitors are usually offered meat. A large lounge and Malcolm's small study are the other principal rooms on the ground floor. The books are kept in check down here, but as one goes up the stairs they begin to appear in corners and behind tables, spilling out of the large book-cases that seem to be everywhere one looks. One case contains multiple copies of most of Malcolm's writings.

He works for much of the time in 'The Ark', a large self-contained building hard by the cottage, which he had built as a study and also as accommodation for family and other visitors. It contains a bed and there is a small kitchen and bathroom. When the family come to stay Malcolm and Kitty retire to the Ark and the family sleep in the house. The main room is spacious and high-ceilinged; one wall is lined with books, and the walls are crammed with photographs and memorabilia. Two of the most recent items to be added are a cartoon by Trog celebrating Muggeridge's eightieth birthday, and a photograph by Jane Bowen of Muggeridge and Alec Vidler on the day that Malcolm and Kitty were received into the Roman Catholic Church. Death-masks of Blaise Pascal and William Blake brood down from the top of the bookcases; several Blake engrav-ings are displayed together by the fireplace. As a minor concession to advancing years, a telephone has recently been installed in the Ark.

Malcolm's day begins early. 'I find nowadays that the time I think most efficiently is between four and five o'clock. I get up and make myself a pot of tea' (the first of many through the day) 'and I sit at my desk, and for about an hour my mind is wonderfully clear.' After breakfasting with Kitty he works again during the morning. At lunch-time there may be visitors and the afternoon be spent in conversation; otherwise, an hour or two more work after lunch, and then he and Kitty will go for a walk. The evenings are relaxed and quiet. They have no television. Malcolm has written voluminously about the evils of the small screen, but even apart from the religious and social implications, he just doesn't like it very much. I asked him if he would be watching Laurence Olivier's much-publicised *King Lear*. He wasn't interested: 'The play is so vast, and Shakespeare is saying such enormous things – and then to see those tiny men walking around inside that little box . . .'

In fact you find, on meeting Malcolm and Kitty, that many aspects of their lifestyle that you had heard of and assumed to be exercises in vigorous self-sacrifice turn out instead to be simply personal preference. They drink camomile tea instead of ordinary tea, but their reason is that they like it better. They neither smoke nor drink, but not out of any self-mortification; they simply don't like cigarettes or alcohol. (Malcolm has said that he no longer smokes because he wants to remain healthy and go on working for as long as possible; nevertheless, he first stopped smoking when several years ago he walked into a room scattered with overflowing ashtrays and gave up tobacco there and then out of sheer disgust. He had been a heavy smoker and drinker.) He rises at four – but only because he finds he works better then. They are not ascetics striving to subdue the flesh. On the contrary, their life is rich and full of

16

enjoyment, and to be in their home is not merely a spiritual and mental satisfaction (which it is); it is a sociable, friendly and accommodating household with no sense of deprivation.

III

The layout of the book requires some explanation. Many of the subjects we talked about were discussed in several sessions, and Malcolm's comments are often drawn from conversations separated by several days. In order to make it clear where this has happened, I have indicated where a major time interval exists between comments. I have of course silently edited where necessary to deal with minor repetitions and so on. In addition, though Malcolm's answers are much more interesting than my questions, I have thought it necessary to include the gist of most of them. In this way Malcolm's remarks are put in the context in which he made them, rather than giving the impression that they are off-the-cuff unprompted observations. Quotations from his books and broadcasts are referenced in the text. Unacknowledged quotations are taken from conversations.

We began with a neat synopsis, outlining exactly what we would talk about and when. It did not work out like that. Malcolm's conversation ranges far and wide, drawing on a vast store of reading, writing and living. You can start to talk about the latest film in the local cinemas, and before you know it he has related it to the decline of the West, the rise of television, ethical standards in twentieth-century England and half-a-dozen other appropriate and illuminating topics. He talks about each of them wittily and provocatively. It makes for an exciting afternoon's conversation, but it ruins a synopsis.

17

The book is instead gathered round several central themes, which are indicated by the chapter headings. The movement is from the general to the particular: chapter one speaks of knowledge about God, chapter two of knowing God personally. The last two chapters of conversation are short; the first because it is a single, virtually unedited extract from a longer conversation; the second, because the subject has been covered by implication throughout the rest of the book.

I have been given a great deal of help by many people in writing this book. My greatest debt, which cannot be repayed, is acknowledged in the dedication.

CHAPTER ONE

Concerning God

Archbishop Anthony Bloom: '*St. Seraphim of Sarov . . .
said that since he knew God he could say it was worth
suffering . . . every moment of one's life, in order to know
[him].*'
Malcolm Muggeridge: 'Of course. Although not a
particular believer myself, I feel that this is so.'

BBC Television programme, 1963.

'The process of creation contains in itself its own
imperfection; the pursuit of perfection is via
imperfection, as the pursuit of spiritual love is via the
physical body . . . This is why there is literature, why
there is art, why there is thought, and how we may know
there is a God – a loving God – whose children we are.'

In conversation with Roy Trevivian, published 1969.

'So, looking, we find him, finding him, we love him . . .'

'Through the eye' (Lecture, 1976)

Questioner: '*How can you say that Christianity is higher or better than atheism?*'
Muggeridge: 'Only because I am a Christian.'

Answering questions at the University of Waterloo, 1978.

Religion's central questions are really the same as those asked by philosophy, and are neatly summarised by philosopher C. E. M. Joad (between whom and Malcolm Muggeridge there are some interesting parallels to be drawn). 'Some of us want to know the meaning of this surprising world in which we find ourselves, to understand the significance and, if possible, to discover the purpose of human life and our own lives in particular. What is the point of life and how ought it to be lived?' The only difference between philosophy and religion at this point is that religion attempts to give absolute answers.

One of the things that Malcolm Muggeridge returns to most often when he talks about his beliefs is his lifelong awareness that there is something outside this world which provides a perspective from which all human, earthly hopes and ambitions seem somewhat preposterous. He shares with C. S. Lewis ('I felt a tremendous sense of identification when reading *Surprised by Joy* . . .') memories of a childhood desire, which Lewis called 'joy' and which others have called 'longing', the end result of which is to make one feel that the world is not one's proper home.

One strange thing I've never been able to account for is that I used to do a very curious thing; I still don't understand it. I used to take a Bible to bed with me, and I used to open it anywhere and have a look at it. And I would feel that somehow by having it open I would be able to derive wisdom and strength and even

20

protection. That was peculiar, because there was nobody in my home who would have suggested that, and the Bible didn't have any place in our family life.

Kitty Muggeridge also traces her religious awareness back to childhood:

> I can't remember ever being an atheist, though I also can't remember thinking very much about it. When I was a child I used to believe very devoutly in God. It was a child's God; I used to pick flowers for him, and I believed that my mother was going to heaven. I used to say to her that if she was going to die, would she take the flowers up with her . . . Nobody taught us that. My mother used to read us Bible stories, but the religious base to our lives was not a strong one. I had that view of God as a child, and as I grew older, I didn't think very much about it.

Though Malcolm's family was avowedly atheistic and Kitty's was not, it was Malcolm who entered his teens with a stronger sense of the existence of God. The environment in which he lived was hardly helpful. The family had no church commitment.

> I occasionally attended a Congregational chapel – there was a very picturesque old man from the Hebrides who was in charge of it. But I never felt any sense of identification with the chapel.

In conversation with Roy Trevivian in 1969 he cheerfully conceded that his reason for going to the chapel was that he wanted to meet girls, rather than that he had any interest in what the white-bearded Dr. Sanderson had to say. It was a social meeting-place so far as Malcolm was concerned, not a place of worship.

But at the same time he was increasingly conscious of an instinctive alienation from the world. 'A stranger in a strange land – that's always been a particularly poignant phrase to me.' For much of his teens it was an undefined awareness of the infinite – 'I always had a feeling . . .', together with an admiration for Christian values quite independent of the institutional Church which his family rejected and in which he had found little except a social life: 'I've always had a sort of love affair with Christianity. I've always thought it was the *best* thing you could be.'

In the *Green Stick*, the first volume of his autobiography, Muggeridge – who was by then (1972) openly speaking as a Christian believer – does not devote many pages to his childhood, and has even less to say about his religious impressions. Most of what he says has to do with his contempt for the 'tame clergymen' who attached themselves to the Labour Party and were, he says, produced by the Party on public occasions as proof of its spiritual bona fides and adherence to the New Testament ethic.

> Of course my father had his connections too. There were connections between the Labour Party and, especially, the Quakers. So we knew for example certain socialist clergy who would sit on the platform and be useful electorally . . . There was a general impression in Croydon and elsewhere in those days, that anyone who was a socialist must also be a free-lover or a libertine; so you had a clergyman to give a touch of respectability to something that might otherwise appear quite disreputable.

Indeed most of his comments on Christianity take the form

of trenchant criticisms of its visible follies and inconsistencies. A parade of weak Christians march through the seventy-odd pages which cover his first sixteen years, and receive the same acid treatment as do the socialists who gathered at his father's home to plan the improvement of the 'working man' (who, Muggeridge remarks, was always conspicuous by his absence from the Saturday-night meetings). Although today he often refers to his childhood awareness of the infinite, it appears that what was happening was that he was rejecting pretence wherever he saw it – in Church or Party – and that whatever his intuitions may have been, they do not add up to a defined belief put forward in its place.

> Do remember that my home was completely agnostic. I heard nothing of the truth. My father and his friends were always talking about socialism, and some sort of wonderful life that was going to come when they and their like took over power. But God Almighty was a figure of fun. They were fond of telling jokes, like Disraeli's comment to Gladstone – 'I don't object to you keeping your trumps up your sleeve, but I do object to you saying God put them there.' That was their attitude. So what interest I had in the Bible and anything to do with God was not derived from the environment in which I lived.

When he was seventeen, Christianity assumed a different importance in his life. 'I didn't in any way crystallise my belief until I got to Cambridge.' Muggeridge's view of his time at Cambridge appears to have changed in the past few years. Ian Hunter, in *Malcolm Muggeridge: a life* (written in 1979), points out the inconsistency between the description of undergraduate life in *The Green Stick* as 'a place of infinite tedium', and the evidence of the letters written at the time in which Muggeridge writes as an energetic and involved student, frustrated only because he could not do more for his college. As Hunter comments, memory is selective. (C. S. Lewis was so critical of *his* old school in *Surprised by Joy* that Lord Hailsham, another old boy, was moved to write to a newspaper in its defence shortly after publication of Lewis's book.) Today Muggeridge speaks quite warmly of Selwyn as a place where he began to meet with and talk with Christians. One of these was Alec Vidler, who today is his oldest and closest friend.

> There was Alec Vidler, and of course there was Selwyn College, which was in those days a Christian college. Chapel was compulsory. I liked it, but pretended to grumble about it, as did everyone else. I was quite consciously stirred up to think about Christianity. Alec belonged to a religious order for Anglican priests – the Oratory of the Good Shepherd. I stayed there for two terms, and of course one was thinking of the possibility of being a Christian – even becoming a monk. The person who influenced me most at the Oratory of the Good Shepherd was Wilfred Knox. They were all Anglo-Catholics, a movement which seems to have all but expired today but which was very strong at Cambridge at the time I was a student.

The shock of leaving the atheistic socialism of his family home in Croydon and suddenly finding himself in a high-church environment may well have been one reason for his interest in entering the priesthood.

> At home churchgoing was not an item in our lives at all. It was a bit of a joke – the Labour Party viewed

24

the Anglican Church as the Tory Party at prayer . . . it was part of the apparatus of the Tory Party, it belonged to the enemy, the 'other people'.

His enthusiasm for the priesthood gradually faded, leaving a strong sense of destiny as yet undefined, and a sense of commitment to Christianity (though he was as sceptical as ever about the Church, and had many arguments with Alec Vidler on the subject).

After leaving Cambridge, Muggeridge went to teach at Union Christian College in south India, at the invitation of one of the staff who had visited Cambridge during his last year. His time at Union College, where he taught a version of Christianity that raised some eyebrows and where his political views also attracted attention, is described in the autobiographies and elsewhere. The comment he has most often made about it in conversation is that while he found it impossible to identify with the Christians there on such matters as prayer for everyday needs, he has the happiest memories of fellowship and friendship with them.

Malcolm Muggeridge considers that by the time he left Union College, he knew who God was. He called himself a Christian; though he had decided against the priesthood, he saw his life in terms of a vocation (though in what precise sense he was not clear); and in his letters to Alec Vidler he spoke often in religious terms. If you ask him today, 'When did you become a Christian?' – this is the period in his life he is most likely to point you to.

The question of when he became a Christian is probably now the one that Malcolm is most often asked. It is often phrased in very specific terms. 'When were you actually converted, and when did you accept Christ as your Saviour?' he was asked in the discussion following one of his lectures on 'Christ and the Media' in 1976. He answered as he has answered many times, discounting any 'Damascus Road' experience, and describing his life as a pilgrimage towards faith. As he often does, he used Bunyan's *Pilgrim's Progress* as an illustration.

The transcript of that evening's discussion does not indicate whether the enquirer was satisfied with the reply. Possibly he or she was not. Phrased as it was, the question invited a reply that talked about a decisive moment of commitment; it implied that a Christian ought to be able to look back to such a moment.

The questioner's uneasiness is understandable. If Muggeridge's life has been a gradual growth into faith, it has hardly been a self-evident one. Many of his pronouncements over the years have been decidedly agnostic, explicitly disowning faith, and speaking of it as a longed-for, but unattained, ideal. As late as 1971, he wrote:

> What is more difficult to convey is the longing one feels to belong to the Church . . . Why not, then? Because for me, it would be fraudulent, and we cannot buy faith . . . with counterfeit urges.

It was a statement about his disillusionment with the visible Church, but it recalled earlier statements pointing to a deepseated agnosticism. In 1964, interviewing himself (!) on BBC's Woman's Hour, he said,

> I certainly find that the dogmas of . . . the Christian religion . . . are to me completely incredible. I can't possibly and could never believe in them.

His writings present the reader with the conundrum; on one hand, certain basic themes appear so often that they were inescapable; and they reflect some of the central pre-

26

occupations of Christianity – the emptiness of earthly power, the supernatural otherness of the spiritual life which is the only perspective from which one can usefully look at the world; the final inability of earthly life to create lasting satisfaction for an individual; the foolishness and cruelty of the other world; and other concepts like them. On the other hand, if this is Christian belief, it is at odds with a great deal of what the Bible says, and it stands opposed to the fellowship of the Church of Christ on earth. Muggeridge's 1966 description of himself as possibly one of those destined to stand for ever outside the Church ringing the bell so that others might come and enter it, sounds a correct Christian humility; but in terms of the New Testament it is plainly silly. The New Testament knows nothing of Christians living out their lives outside the Church, least of all acting as exhorters of the faithful.

It's understandable that many Christians in the late sixties (especially evangelicals) received the impression that Malcolm Muggeridge had been 'converted'. Biblically speaking, there are two definitions of what it means to become a Christian; one is a change of life evidencing a change of heart, and the other is a spoken witness to the fact that one has become a 'new creature'. This is not merely an 'evangelical' formulation. It is the recorded experience of Christians through the centuries that there was a time when they did not believe, but that they came to do so; whether, like John Bunyan, in a moment of crisis, or whether, like the contemplative monks of the fourteenth century, over a long period, the fact is recorded that their lives changed. The fact that it is recorded at all is part of their spoken testimony.

In the late sixties, Malcolm Muggeridge's writings and pronouncements began to reiterate what was essentially a new theme. Suddenly he was identifying himself with

Christians, not in isolated phrases, but repeatedly. Further-more, after a writing lifetime of questioning and scepticism, he was now affirming and asserting. By reputation a cynic and a puller-down, he was now in the business, it seemed, of building up.

Having said that, it must be added that any attempt to trace a chronology of growing commitment in Muggeridge's various pronouncements is ill-advised. Certainly he had moved on from the position he claimed in the fifties when, as Editor of *Punch*, he replied to criticism from the Archbi-shop of Canterbury and remarked 'I am, alas, not myself a believing Christian. I wish I were.' But those who seized on occasional statements which appeared to confirm Muggeridge as a newly-arrived sheep within the Christian fold were liable to be disconcerted by the discovery that a week later he would be writing as sardonically as ever about religion, the Church and other aspects of Christianity.

However, one book represented something quite new in his writings. *Jesus Rediscovered* (1969) was a compilation of Muggeridge's writings on Christ and Christianity. It became a best-seller, and is today still in the best-seller lists. He receives two or three letters a day from people who have been helped by it.

From the point of view of orthodox Christian belief, *Jesus Rediscovered* leaves numerous ends untied. The pieces it contains cover a span of several years, and there is a discernible development. The famous address to the St. Andrews students was for many people the first realisation that he was now speaking as a Christian; there are essays and broadcast scripts, often going over the familiar ground of the transitoriness of the world, his unease about the Church, his ridiculing of human pretensions. The collec-tion ends with an extended interview with Roy Trevivian, in which Muggeridge spoke frankly about issues which he had not dealt with previously; his capacity as a father, his relationship with God, and his views about death. The book leaves you with one thing strongly in the memory. Muggeridge proclaimed himself to be a Christian because he felt that he now lived the kind of life which would not discredit the gospel. He had resisted identifying himself as a follower of Jesus before, because he felt himself unworthy. Now he felt that his life could bear scrutiny to some extent.

Anything more likely to raise the hackles of the orthodox biblical Christian can scarcely be imagined. The idea that one can actually be worthy of the name of Christian is repellent to a large body of Christians. 'Worm theology' or not, the evangelical tradition is not the only strand of the Christian Church that has always resisted the idea that one can merit salvation or that Christianity is only available to those who live a life worthy of it. Predictably, while thousands found the book of enduring and profound value, thousands more were suspicious of Muggeridge's new-found faith.

The years since *Jesus Rediscovered* both confirmed and contradicted these reactions. Those who were suspicious of Muggeridge found plenty to be worried about in his repeated affirmation that the Church was a lost cause, that God was not interested in the daily lives of his creatures, and that the Bible contained 'imaginative truth' rather than literal fact. Those on the other hand who found the book profoundly helpful found that Muggeridge returned to certain themes with increasing fervour: the certainty that love is the driving force behind the universe, that in Christ the insane paradoxes of life find a perspective and a resolution, and the belief that life in the world, far from being all that human existence is, is really only a brief interlude in it.

His next book was *Something Beautiful for God*, a luminous celebration of the work of Mother Teresa of Calcutta and her work among incurables. His text was accompanied by photographs which were themselves suffused with a radiant spirituality (and were, incidentally, a miracle in themselves – there had not, according to Muggeridge, been enough light to film by). *Something Beautiful for God* lacks the combativeness of the earlier books. It is written in a state of spiritual shock, while its author was still stunned by the charisma and faith of its subject. Muggeridge speaks as an outsider, observing the Church as a visible healing and transforming power in the world, but unable to be involved himself. Much of the book consists of his apologia to Mother Teresa for his inability to enter the Church. So, once again, readers were faced with the double spectacle of Muggeridge pleading the case of God and Mother Teresa passionately and powerfully, while at the same time remaining agnostic and aloof in areas which many would consider crucial.

Paul, Envoy Extraordinary appeared in 1972. The most significant thing about this script of Muggeridge's televised tour of St. Paul's routes with Alec Vidler is the role of Dr. Vidler. As a book it is less than successful, probably a good indication of the effectiveness of the original film; it is like watching with the picture turned off. The book begins with a lengthy tribute by Muggeridge to Vidler and ends with an authoritative and incisive analysis of Paul's achievements, also by Vidler. In between, the two friends tour the Eastern Mediterranean, Muggeridge's instincts for good television documentary and his acute sense of the right questions to ask providing a foil for Vidler's scholarship. As part of the Muggeridge canon it is a very slight book. As an indication of Vidler's influence on him as counsellor and spiritual guide, it is extremely significant.

Following two volumes of autobiography, tellingly entitled *Chronicles of Wasted Time* and stopping before the time we are now talking about, Muggeridge published in 1975 *Jesus, the Man Who Lives.*

He had previously scripted three half-hour television programmes, shot in the Holy Land, on the life of Christ. In the published version (*A Life of Christ*, 1968, later included in *Jesus Rediscovered*), he gave as his reason for writing:

> All I have cared about is the living presence of Christ; the life he lived, and the death he died, and the unique salvation he offers to a distracted world today.

The *Life of Christ* was a pamphlet of 32 pages. *Jesus, the Man Who Lives*, is a substantial book. It is a summing up of the affirmations of the previous few years, and faced with an awesome subject Muggeridge produced what is arguably his best book. Described by Ian Hunter as 'surprisingly orthodox', it is a portrait in broad strokes of a Jesus who is at once recognisable as the Christ of the Gospels, but also is urgently relevant to present times. The closing pages, with their conclusion that Jesus lives because Jesus rose from the dead, are among the finest Muggeridge has written.

In the last few years he has written on a number of Christian subjects. His well-known views on the media were trenchantly stated in *Christ and the Media* (in which John Stott, the chairman of the original lectures, speaks of Muggeridge as a 'true prophet', and in which Muggeridge's central message was, 'Stay with the reality of Christ'); his views on euthanasia and related ethical issues found a vehicle in the play, *Sentenced to Life*, which he co-authored; and in *A Third Testament* (1976) he gives sympathetic accounts of his choice of 'God's spies', again based on a television series. He has continued to appear in the media, where he has continued to promote a Christian viewpoint on any subject on which he is asked to speak.

He is today one of the most articulate and prophetic Christian voices. But if it is suggested to him that this is all a rather recent development, he will point you back to his time at Cambridge and in south India.

Ever after, being at Cambridge and certainly in India later teaching at the Christian college there, I felt myself to be a Christian. But not a good one. A bad one.

Did you ever get to a point where you thought you were a good one?

No . . . No, I'm afraid not. But I'm better than I was.

CHAPTER TWO

Knowing God

Come, not to study the history of God's divine action, but to be its object; not to learn what it has achieved throughout the centuries and still does, but simply to be the subject of its operation.

Jean-Pierre de Caussade, *Self-abandonment to Divine Providence* (translated by Kitty Muggeridge as *The Sacrament of the Present Moment*).

The manifestation of God in the flesh, the Evangelists set down by way of a history; the apostle [Paul] goes farther, and finds a deep mystery in it, and for a mystery commends it to us. Now there is a difference between these two, many – this for one; that a man may hear a story, and never wash his hands; but a mystery requires both the hands and heart to be clean that shall deal with it.

Lancelot Andrewes, *XVII Sermons on the Nativity*, III.

Knowing God is more than knowing about him; it is a matter of dealing with him as he opens up to you, and being dealt with by him as he takes knowledge of you.

Knowing about him is a necessary precondition of trusting in him, but the width of our knowledge about him is no gauge of our knowledge of him.

J. I. Packer, *Knowing God*.

. . . I should be proud and happy to call myself a Christian; to be able to measure myself against that immeasurably high standard of human values and human behaviour. In this I take comfort from another saying of Pascal, thrown out like a lifeline to all sceptical minds throughout the ages – that whosoever looks for God has found him.

Malcolm Muggeridge, 'What I believe' (1966).

One prays in the same sort of way that one talks to somebody one is fond of . . . it brings you closer to him.

Malcolm Muggeridge in conversation, Easter 1983.

It is relatively easy to work out from Malcolm's writings whether he believes in God; he is well-known as a champion of the faith and a brilliant opponent of anybody who dismisses the idea that God might exist. If one draws a middle line through the variety of statements he has made over the years, there is no doubt that for many years past that has been his position.

We took this question as the starting point of our conversations. If God exists, I asked Malcolm, then does he expect human beings to do anything about that fact?

What I've found interesting in your writings and in our conversations is the balance between the Bible's emphasis

that when we talk about 'knowing God' we can only use
human terms to describe something which is super-human;
and the testimony of Christians down the ages, including
yourself, to the fact that personal knowledge of God is
possible.

Yes. But only through the incarnation. That's the thing
about it, it was essentially an act of mercy, whereby
people could know God, in the only possible way: by
God becoming a man. And I see that as the supreme
illustration of God's understanding of creation. The only
way he could really communicate with human beings
was by becoming one.

Of course there's a degree of symbolism involved. But
still the fact of the incarnation is the centre of the whole
business, and it does enable us to know God.

What does that mean to you – to 'know God'?

Well, to know God means first to be aware, however
vaguely, of the purpose of your existence as part of
God's creation. Unless you know God, you can't
understand that.

Do you mean the special purpose of God for yourself, or his
purpose for mankind as a whole?

Both. Insofar as you know God (and even then it's
imperfect, Cardinal Newman says somewhere that 'the
words we use are merely to convey what can't be
conveyed'), through knowing him we can achieve what
alone makes life possible. And that is, to know what his
purpose is towards us. Take that away, and life means
nothing at all.

That really is the whole essence of it, isn't it? One wants
to please God, one wants to fulfil God's purpose. That's

the beginning and end of the whole thing. I find Simone Weill extremely helpful here. She was very fond of the phrase 'Waiting on God' (which is a different matter to 'Waiting for God'). One can in humility and patience wait on God, and in that get some idea of how one should live, how one should conduct oneself, what are the real things, what are the fantasy things.

'Waiting on God' – in other words you as it were try, to lay aside your ego, to lay aside whatever vestiges of things like carnality still exist in you, and in that state, with your mind dwelling upon things that are good, things that are creative and not destructive, loving and not malignant, universal and not particular – things like that – you are in that state of mind where you do have some sort of notion of what God wants. And then you rejoice accordingly.

But what precisely did 'waiting on God' mean? For example, I asked, did it mean that you wait for God to communicate, to say something specific, in terms that are directly relevant to you?

Not in the sense of being able to hear words spoken; I've never experienced that. In my experience it's more the realisation of a state of mind, which makes you sensitive to God's purposes; this 'waiting on God' means putting yourself in a relationship. And that relationship leads you into a certain way of life, certain values, certain behaviour. It's more a form of intuition than a concrete 'word of command' from God, you might say.

God might communicate when you are reading a book, for example, and not only when reading the Bible; two lines of George Herbert, something like that, suddenly epitomise truth.

This approach has sometimes led people to label Malcolm a 'Quietist'. Quietism is an approach to Christianity and the spiritual life which usually has had an exaggerated emphasis on the principle of 'inner quiet', and teaches that the Christian's highest duty is to passively contemplate God. There is hardly any emphasis on the idea that one should, by doing things, make an active response to God's love.

Because of some comments made at various times and usually taken out of context, Malcolm Muggeridge has sometimes been thought to follow the more extreme kinds of Quietism. But the term 'Quietism' itself includes a number of different viewpoints, and if the description is to be applied to Muggeridge, it would have to be in terms of the Quietism of somebody like François Fénelon in the early eighteenth century (who was, with Madame Guyon his companion, a strong influence on William Cowper and other early evangelicals).

Fénelon made a careful distinction between 'true quietude', which (he argued) is something which the Christian receives from the Holy Spirit, and passive 'perpetual contemplation' which he regarded as impossible. He stressed the necessity of 'spiritual co-operation' between the believer and his God, the impossibility of making contemplation and interior quiet merely a refuge from the sins of the flesh, and the difference between 'interested' and 'disinterested' love.

In conversation, Malcolm endorses the concept of 'disinterested love', though without referring it to any particular writer apart from Simone Weill. His attitudes to prayer, to guidance, and to most areas of the Christian life are profoundly affected by the idea that the greatness of God is such that it would be 'almost impertinent' to come to him simply to get something you wanted.

You have written that the notion that the Creator of the universe should take an interest in, say, how you were going to spend the afternoon, would be an impertinence. Do you still believe that?

I don't think that sort of thing would be a source of concern on high, no.

Is it something you would pray about?

I'm not very happy praying for specific things for myself. My ultimate prayer, which transcends all other prayers, is 'Thy will be done.' And we have that beautiful prayer of St. Chrysostom, 'Lord, give us grace at this time that we may with one accord make our common supplication unto thee . . .' That I like very much. It's a beautiful prayer, and perhaps it is the one most expedient for us. It gives an open cheque to the Lord.

It was a theme that recurred several times in conversation. Prayer is something which is extremely important to Malcolm and his views are not as simple as they at first appear.

What about cases of genuine perplexity?

Well – we're always bound to be perplexed – perplexity is as it were a condition of life.

But on a day-to-day basis? For example, if something was a matter of deep anxiety and concern to you?

The only prayer I pray for myself now really is Lord,

let me go on working . . . I've a few things I want to say still, a few undertakings I've given, and I find that now one is old it gets harder to work. For other people? Well, suppose one of my grandchildren is ill. I love that child, I would do anything for that child not to be ill, would dispose of any possession I might have; I hope that I might even be willing to sacrifice myself if that would help . . . But to actually ask God to make him better? It seems that that would be troubling God about the matter when we should have faith that he will do what's right and best for the child.

Opinions like these have earned Muggeridge another label from some of his critics, who call him a fatalist who believes that God will do what God wants to do, and nobody can change matters at all. But further conversations made it clear that Malcolm is very far from believing that.

One thing he is very definite about is that he does not regard his own feelings on prayer as absolutes for all Christians, and certainly would not say that somebody who had a different view was in some way on spiritually dangerous ground.

I remember that when I was in India, I stayed in a house with a number of evangelical Christians, and they were the most delightful people. And when they prayed, it was as if they were producing shopping lists for God. And why not?

But I myself could not do that. Though again, people do ask one to pray for them. And I always do, in case it may be helpful.

Is it partly a question of language, of defining what prayer is?

Yes. You know if you are agonising about whether something or other should happen, God knows that you are. And you hope that all other things being equal things will be resolved as you hope they will be.

Is the passage in the New Testament relevant here, where Jesus makes it clear that the importunate woman was heard because she asked repeatedly?

I think that's a very fascinating parable. Like so many of them, it's a worldly story. I like them the better for it. But it doesn't lead me to believe that I have to be importunate. Jesus is saying that the people who get what they want in this world are importunate. Just as he's saying, about the unjust steward, that the children of darkness know more about the mammon of unrighteousness than the children of light. Those are true statements, and I admire him for making them, because they're very daring things to be saying.

Perhaps more relevant is the story of the Centurion who came to Jesus for help and said, 'You don't even need to come to my house . . .'

Absolutely. I find that man a very sympathetic man. He's really saying to our Lord, 'I know quite well that if you consider it right to bring that child to life, you will. And it doesn't matter whether you're there or not there.'

I don't think that there is a terribly fundamental problem here, because I believe it is partly a matter of temperament, and partly, as you were saying, of how you express these things.

I think that if you fill your whole soul with this idea of 'Thy will be done' and that nothing else matters at all but that God's will be done and that I should fall into it, then these other matters do pale into insignificance. When St. Teresa of Avila says, 'Our life in this world is like a night in a second class hotel' I agree with her absolutely; and I think it's almost insulting to God and man to suggest that trivial events should give rise to deep concern on his part.

So you yourself pray a very embrasive prayer, but if somebody else preferred to pray the other way – 'compile a shopping list' –

I don't think there would be anger on high about that. Mother Teresa has a rather different way of seeing this. I remember when a very dear friend was dying she asked me to ask Mother Teresa to pray for her, which of course she did. And she wrote one of her marvellous letters back which gave the impression that all the sisters were going at it hammer and tongs bombarding God with prayer on my friend's behalf. 'But if,' added Mother Teresa, 'the time has come now for her to go home, would you please ask her to remember me to Jesus and his mother when she gets there?' Now, that's absolutely marvellous, and completely characteristic of her, but it isn't how I myself would be able to see it.

Do you think it matters, that it's possible that either you or the person with the 'shopping list' might have got it quite wrong and be praying in quite the wrong way? Or do you think that God allows us to define for ourselves how we relate to him?

Yes, I do. I personally think that it would be a mistake to pray other than the way I do myself, but it wouldn't worry me. What lies behind all this – and I've often thought about it – is this. When we know (as we no

41

doubt will some day) what were the transcendental verities of our existence, we shall find that our attempts to convey or express our ideas of God and heaven and so on were no more than the writing of children before they knew their letters. And therefore the particular idiom in which any man chooses to approach his creator will be so utterly beside the point if and when we know what is truly signified, that it's not a matter of major importance.

So we might be with Pentecostal people; they have their own way of addressing God. Or we may find our way into an old-style Catholic Mass. Equally, these are people trying to communicate with God – honestly, sincerely, beautifully. They can only do what is all any of us can do, which is, to use the idiom of a mortal in time to communicate with a holy, spiritual Being in eternity. Which will obviously be inadequate, just as I would expect some little child to be in addressing his parents.

When I asked him to expand on this, Malcolm was reluctant to extend the father-child image.

The Bible uses that image quite often, doesn't it – do you feel it helps us in this whole business of God and time? Because the father is not really terribly interested in what the child is doing. For instance if my daughter is cutting out a paper doll and she accidentally cuts one of its arms off, I sit down with her and help her to work out another way of doing what she wants. But it's of no real interest to me. I haven't the slightest interest in cutting dolls out of paper. I do it because I'm her father and she asks me to.

I can accept the image, but to me it would seem preposterous to involve God in the trivial details of our earthly existence. On the other hand, that's purely a personal thing. I can be perfectly comfortable with other Christians who may have a different way of praying.

Underlying Malcolm's attitude to prayer is a strong theological distinction between God the Father and Jesus Christ. Though he insists that theological niceties are of no interest to him, he preserves the distinction, with his usual interest in precise language, between God who is Spirit and Jesus Christ who became man.

But don't we see Christ in his life on earth doing things for other people, not just to teach them about himself or to teach them lessons about God, but out of gratuitous kindness? Turning the water into wine was certainly a demonstration of the power of God, but it was also a very kind gesture to people who were in a highly embarrassing social position! And that very fact would indicate that whatever else God is, there is an element of gratuitous kindness in him. People ask Jesus to do things – Jesus' mother asked him to deal with the wine problem. . .

But now you are talking about the incarnation, and I must say to you that the marvel of the incarnation is that Jesus became a man. When he becomes a part of the Godhead I can know that man because he was once himself a man. I know him through the time when he was on earth; I recognise that it is possible to be with him on earth. But it would never seem to me that this would involve his getting preoccupied about the devices and desires (to use the prayerbook phrase) of our life here on earth. Its particulars are not really important to him. It's only a tiny interlude in our existence.

In other words we have the fellowship of Jesus because he was incarnate, he was a man. But with God, we haven't the faintest idea, really, about him. The word simply means we recognise there is a God, but the minute we begin to try to define him, it seems to me that we're at sea. Except for this marvellous thing of the incarnation.

A criticism of Malcolm which is often made is that much of what he says about human existence can be disregarded as the meditations of an elderly man who is suffering an advanced form of world-weariness. This is especially so when he talks about ethical issues; a common reaction to his stand on permissiveness and pornography is that he is someone who, too old to enjoy such things any more, is now sniping petulantly at those who still can. But this argument ignores the fact that Muggeridge has been sounding that particular clarion call for many years; and that whatever his view of the transitoriness of this world's splendours may or may not be, he enjoys the world more than many of his critics do.

Nevertheless, his perspective on life is necessarily influenced by the fact that he is, as he repeatedly reminds us, bound to leave it before long. This affects the way he thinks about God and the way he relates to him, particularly in prayer.

The prayer which really comprises all other prayers is the phrase in our Lord's prayer: 'Thy will be done'. All that one can want in life is that God's will be done. All that one can ask is to have some idea of what fosters that will or what opposes or precludes it. But when you come to the little minutae of an existence, such as whether I should go to Timbuctoo as a correspondent or stay in London . . . I have never been able to think that that is a matter with which I should bother God. I don't think it matters to him whether I go to Timbuctoo or not. Some Christians assume that every single thing in life is of enormous interest to God. From their point of view they may be right.

But I don't attach great importance to the particulars of our life on earth – whether we're successful or whether we're failures, whether we're attractive or whether we're unattractive – all those things seem to me to belong merely to time. And as I approach the end of my life it seems to me more and more clear that the importance to be attached to them is greatly exaggerated.

One can see the critics' case; the two volumes of autobiography already published, together with Ian Hunter's life of Muggeridge to complete the story, are crowded with events and people. Some of the most dramatic episodes of modern history are featured in them. Whatever his views now, he has not always given the impression of a world-wearied contemplative, convinced of the unimportance of the works of time.

What about somebody, though, who's twenty-five? Is what you are saying absolute for the whole of life?

It is and it isn't. It's a conclusion that becomes confirmed as you grow old, but it's a conclusion I arrived at long ago.

I put forward the example of a young man or woman faced with the choice between a brilliant academic career, work as a probation officer in down-town Glasgow, or service abroad as a missionary:

His overall prayer may well be, 'Thy will be done.' But he isn't likely to think of these three options as irrelevancies of existence. He is going to want to know which of the three is going to further God's will most effectively.

Again, I can understand that; but as you know from the things I have written about my life, I've never myself made any plans. I've just acted day by day or year by year, and it's never seemed to matter very much.

You called your autobiography The Chronicles of Wasted Time . . .

That is a phrase from Shakespeare's sonnets, and in Elizabethan English it means used-up time, wasting like a candle wastes.

But I wanted it to mean both things because really I have wasted an enormous amount of time.

You say somewhere that you may feel you have achieved nothing, and are conscious only of the feeling of your own inadequacy.

This is true. I think that is the lesson of human life. Jesus said 'Unless you hate your life in this world, you can't get along in eternity.' Well, people might say that that's a mistranslation, that something's gone wrong there; but I believe it. Really the word 'hate' is not nearly so important and momentous as is suggested, not only in past times, but specifically in modern times when the individual ego is considered to be so tremendously important. And I've never felt that I would wish to bother God, as it were, with questions which to me really are not very important.

You use the words 'bother' and 'concern'. But surely a father

46

is not concerned because he has to be but because he chooses to be – out of his grace, if you like.

I've nine grandchildren, you know. But I've never thought it to be a matter of life or death whether they were going to do one thing and be successful, or do another thing else and be failures. The particularities of life are greatly exaggerated.

St. Francis didn't give any thought about what he was going to do or where he was going to go. He just wanted to tell people about Jesus.

I asked Malcolm what place prayer had in his daily life. The question of how to pray occupies many Christian writers; it's something many Christians find difficult and sometimes disappointing. Some of the best-known believers in history have said that of all parts of the Christian life they found it most difficult. What was Malcolm's experience of prayer?

If your only prayer is 'Thy will be done', and if you feel personally reluctant to bother God with shopping lists, does this mean that praying is not a lengthy business for you?

No, I pray now more than I've ever prayed! But one prays in the same way that one talks to somebody one is fond of – because it brings one nearer to them. I don't want to ask any particular favours of my Creator . . . though sometimes of course when you are very distraught and forget that, then you do ask for favours . . .

Prayer – I think it is the most marvellous thing! And for me at any rate you have to be regular to do it – I mean every morning and evening and so on. Kitty and I always say matins and evensong each day, and more

on Sundays. The services in the Book of Common Prayer
are wonderful. They say everything one wants to say
. . . and the Psalms, I must have read them twenty
times or more, and I never get tired of them.

CHAPTER THREE

Jesus

Only the disciples see the risen one. Only blind faith
has sight here.
Dietrich Bonhoeffer, *Christology.*

The Christian faith is the most exciting drama that ever
staggered the imagination of man – and the dogma *is* the
drama . . . The plot pivots upon a single character, and
the whole action is the answer to a single central
problem: what think ye of Christ?
Dorothy L. Sayers, *The Greatest Drama Ever Staged.*

How, then, is God himself, very God of very God, to
be found and loved? . . . The simple fact is that to be
truly loved God has to become a man without thereby
ceasing to be God. Hence Jesus, who provides the
possibility of loving God through, and in, him, and, as
part of the same process, of loving other men, our
neighbours, through, and in, him. Thus the two
commandments become one; to be celebrated in a man
– Jesus – who dies, and sanctified in a man – also Jesus
– who goes on living.

Malcolm Muggeridge, *Jesus, the Man who Lives.*

There are many religious pundits who will happily theorise for hours about God, but will suddenly become abrupt and taciturn if the conversation turns to Jesus Christ. To talk about God is undemanding; one can broaden into ethics, philosophise about the nature of the Deity, affirm the creation – all without actually involving any personal commitment or opening up the possibility that the Supreme Being of the cosmos might conceivably have some sort of claim on one's individual life and conduct. Talking about Jesus is different. You are always liable to find doors in the universe opening and that uncomfortable presence staring back. You cannot take a bus ride from Jerusalem to Bethlehem without passing lumps of rock on which the Creator may well have sat. He is no Divine Essence silently keeping the universe in order. He became a living man, and in him God has spoken.

For Malcolm Muggeridge the incarnation is the central meaning of history. It is not possible to talk to him for very long about God without the conversation turning inexorably to this event, which Malcolm sees as the heart of the drama of history, the key to the 'great code', which William Blake suggested would unlock the fearful symmetry of the universe.

And the core of the incarnation is for him the Resurrection, the climax of the drama. In the Resurrection, Jesus triumphs over death and lives; and he can therefore be known. And just as there is a difference between knowing about God and knowing God, so in the same way Malcolm draws a distinction between knowing facts about Jesus and subscribing to Jesus' ethical teaching, and being 'with' or 'in' Christ.

You have often in conversation talked about 'being with Christ', which is something you say is possible in this life.

50

But in what sense is a Christian 'with Christ' differently to somebody who is inspired by Christ's teachings, tries to live by them, but does not believe that Jesus is God?

The Christian is 'with Christ' because of the Resurrection. The Resurrection is an absolutely essential part of it all – and the least believed part of Christian doctrine. I do find many of these things difficult to explain. But for me the key to it all is the notion which appears a great deal in my writings and in my talking: that life is a drama, and that for Christians it is the drama of the birth, life, death and resurrection of Jesus Christ. All that happens is essential to that drama.

Take a thing like the virgin birth – it's extremely difficult to explain it to people; but to me it is quite clear that if you accept the miracle of the incarnation, if you accept that Jesus is both God and man, then as man he must be like other men, and as God he must be unlike other men. It is necessary that it should be so. Mary was the mother of Jesus, she suckled him, looked after him, and loved him; but at the same time, because he was also God, even when he was in Mary's womb he had not arrived there by the same process that would have been needed if he had been only man.

The dogma of the Christian faith is largely expressed in terms of Christ's humanity or of his Godhood. It is more difficult to formulate the idea of him being both God and man. Take the Crucifixion, for example. If Jesus is only God then the Crucifixion is quite meaningless, because God does not suffer on a cross. If he was only man, it is equally unreasonable to believe it – a man

51

who was able to be re-appear after he had been crucified?

We have then this extraordinary happening, and we can only understand it if we see it as a drama. Then we can understand it. Then it is real.

And there will come a time (by your reckoning not too far ahead!), when after death you will see Christ in reality, with your own eyes –

Yes, insofar as I can understand; but also I equally know that when I find myself a spirit as well, and am no longer this strange combination – it is a complete mystery to know what things will be like then.

Looking forward to that time, Malcolm, even acknowledging how little one knows of it in advance, are there any aspects of that future, perfect relationship with Christ which you would feel you have already tasted?

What I know now is that Christ is there to strengthen me, hearten me, and enable me to understand God.

By his example? Or in another way?

Not by example. Because he is a part of the drama in which I am involved. He is the leading actor, if you like. And that is crucially important.

Can I put an example to you? If I am depressed about something, I can sit with my wife and talk about it, and she both comforts and advises me. In other words there are specific ways in which the relationship shows itself, there are actual things she does. Does the strengthening and heartening which Jesus gives work like that? Suppose you had great sadness. In what way would you expect Christ to minister to that sadness?

He would certainly minister to it, but not in the same way your wife would. She is a fellow human being. But Jesus does it precisely because he is both God and man. Therefore his comforts, and the enlightenments he gives, are more than any beloved fellow human being could give. Not because he loves more, necessarily, but because of this fact, that he is God and man, he is eternal – and we belong to time.

So is there any distinction, then, any different relationship, between when you pray to Jesus Christ and when you pray to God the Father?

Yes, in the sense that Christ is in the position of having been incarnate, and so he both understands everything about mortal existence but is himself more than mortal.

So although I would not myself feel it appropriate to go to Christ with a 'shopping list', it would be perfectly permissible to do so. Because of the incarnation.

But even then – as Newman said – even as we are talking like this, we are really only talking in allegories. It's the best we can do, being human, living in time; but it's good that we should remember that we can never have any absolute knowledge. We can never begin to understand the Trinity, for instance. But we can have faith, we can say that the concept of the Trinity is a mystery to us, but it's true; and the light that we get when we are thinking about it comes to us via Christ.

What is the role of the Holy Spirit in this?

I've often thought about that. And I think that the Holy Spirit is simply the expression of God's love as it spreads and incorporates everything that there is. To reduce it to its simplest terms: There is God, whom we agree we do not know and are not even supposed to know. Then there is the incarnation, whereby God becomes man and we know him. But there is also this marvellous thing that the incarnation brought into the world, whereby the whole of creation is suffused with the spirit of the incarnation. And that is the Holy Spirit.

Do you think of the Holy Spirit as being personal?

All-pervading . . . You can love someone as a person. You can love someone because they convey a special understanding of what life is about. But you can also love someone because they spread round themselves the love that they express and live by . . . Take Mother Teresa; she has spread about her the spirit of love, and in earthly terms that is like the Holy Spirit.

And it's not by chance that the Holy Spirit is called 'the Comforter'. Because that eternal and everlasting presence is the ultimate comfort which enables us to support and confront the contradictions and limitations of our existence.

What about the role of the Holy Spirit in making the Scriptures clear to us?

I would think that that came into it.

And you know, we use the idea in our everyday language. We say 'There's a wonderful spirit in this house,' maybe, because whatever it is enables us to see things not in earthly terms but in eternal terms – and that is the Holy Spirit. And we are aware when we lose touch with the Holy Spirit – the terrible desolation, of suddenly being nothing but a piece of flesh in time.

I see these three – God, Jesus Christ, the Holy Spirit –

very distinctly, and they seem to me to be absolutely essential for us to understand what the New Testament is all about. And the key word is that word 'Comforter'. It was Jesus' own word. 'I shall send the Comforter.' How are we comforted? Because the Holy Spirit explains to us that mortal, we are immortal; that though sinful and weak, we are aware of sinlessness.

One thing I find very interesting is that it is impossible to find a pronoun for the Holy Spirit. He is not 'he' in the sense that Jesus Christ is called 'he', for Jesus was incarnate. The Holy Spirit is the Comforter. And there have been times in my life when I have been aware of the Holy Spirit – that sudden sense that comes to you in crisis, when your heart is broken, telling you that this is only a tiny thing, and that reality is infinite. 'The cloud of unknowing' – that is a good image for the Holy Spirit, this extraordinary cloud which comes from eternity and cannot be known.

I asked Malcolm whether the fact that one knows God only through Christ meant that there was a difference between 'knowing God' and 'knowing Christ' – whether, in fact, he had moved on from the first, in his early days of God-awareness, to the second, later in life?

I don't think so. The two are so inextricably related you can't separate them. You could say, I suppose, 'Was there ever a time when you knew God and didn't know Christ?' – but I don't think you can have one without the other. To me you can't be a Christian and know God if you don't know Christ – and vice-versa.

Has your coming to know Christ involved any element of confrontation, or has it simply been a gradual coming to

*understanding? You have here Christ, whom you have
described as a very remarkable man, quite apart from his
divinity. Have you ever been challenged by that man to the
extent that your life turned round as a result?*

I'm sure there have been such occasions. Meeting and
talking with people, for example, one might often have
some whole new direction opened up.

Something Beautiful for God *seemed to me to be a book
of confrontation.*

Yes, you could use that word. My whole understanding
of what a Christian is was enlarged. Of course, that
happens almost all the time.

It is exactly the same as when one falls in love with
another human being. One might be asked – 'When
did you fall in love with her?' And it's difficult to say.
But the question really is, 'Do you love her more now
than you used to?'

It develops.

*There must have been a point when you selected that woman
out of all other women.*

Well, all these things happen in different ways, even
conversion. Even on the Damascus Road we don't know
what went before; perhaps the experience simply
crystallised a process. We don't know what doubts and
questions were going through Paul's mind as he was
persecuting the Christians. Certainly the dramatic
conversion doesn't preclude a considerable process
beforehand of working things out.

He watched Stephen's martyrdom . . .

Exactly. That would have been a time when his mind was exercising itself.

We returned to the subject of conversion on another occasion. I was asking Malcolm what advice he would give to somebody who had read his books and wanted to know how to become a Christian.

It seems to me that if we're going to talk about your discipleship then the thing one wants to avoid is that one portrays it as an ongoing development that begins with your earliest awareness and just matures till now. Because if one did that, then someone might say, 'All I need to do to be a disciple like Malcolm Muggeridge is to stay where I am and ripen!'

What I want to put to you is that someone might read your books and say, 'Good, this is the kind of faith I want; how do I go about getting it?' What would you say to somebody, for example, who shared your own disillusionment with socialism and said to you, 'I agree with your critique of the socialist ideal, and I can see from your writings that you have found a different way; how do I follow that way myself?'

Almost exactly that question has been put to me. And I would say: read the Gospels; read the writings of Christian mystics, Christian teachers; follow Christ's way; and everything will be all right.

It's possible that somebody listening to you as you say that might assume that you are describing a 'salvation by works' – that you are saved by things you do, by merit. Whereas in your writings, it's obviously richer than that.

No, I'm not really advocating that. The basic thing is

to find Christ, which is what the evangelicals are talking about. In other words, to establish a relationship with Christ which will enable you to fulfil the Christian life as he envisaged it, insofar as it's possible for anyone to do that. And that is open to anyone to do, whatever his circumstances. Solzhenitsen finds the possibility in the Gulag, and rejoices to have found it and remarks that he could not have found it anywhere else in the USSR, and therefore it was the greatest blessing of his life that he was put in the Gulag.

But you see I don't think there's any kind of standard formula. I think this is a pilgrimage, which each individual has to work out, though he can get a great deal of help. But mostly not from fellow-humans, really.

It's not a salvation of works. I had in mind your picture of the man disillusioned with socialism, saying 'You seem to think there's a Christian alternative, how do I get at it?' And I would think it right to start him off by reading the Gospels and adjusting himself to the Christian perspective . . . and then this living Christ is to be found.

What practical changes would you expect finding the living Christ would make in that individual's life?

I would expect to find joy coming to him. Because he would be released from the dismal situation of having believed that if everyone had the vote, or if an Act of Parliament were passed – something like that – then things would get better. He would be freed from the desolation of finding that that never works . . . The simplest expression of it, which I've often used, is that 'the mighty are put down from their seats, and the humble and weak exalted', but then the humble and weak are mighty and they have to be put down, in other words it's an endless process. But you can find reality and you can find what's meant by love and you can find truth and through Christ you can relate yourself to God, irrespective of all those other things.

CHAPTER FOUR

Sin, Evil and Suffering

Who in heart not ever kneels
Neither sin nor Saviour feels.

George Herbert, *The Temple*.

Miserable man! A toad is a bag of poison, and a spider
is a blister of poison, and yet a toad and a spider cannot
poison themselves; man hath a dram of poison, original-
sin, in an invisible corner, we know not where, and he
cannot choose but poison himself and all his actions with
that . . .

John Donne, Sermon XIII.

Malcolm Muggeridge's views on evil and suffering are
sometimes misinterpreted. His insistence that all of life and
all of human history is a drama, in which each individual
and each event has a place and a part to play, can sometimes
appear to be mere fatalism, a belief that if we were all
actors in a play that has been written already, there is no
point in trying to do things any differently.

But it is surprising how many writers have used the
image of the drama, and how common a theme it is in

61

Christian writing and teaching. A standard response to the question 'Why does God allow suffering?' is often, 'Because the author only comes to stage at the end of the play' – in other words, if he comes on sooner, the play cannot continue. Similarly, the question 'Why are people not incapable of doing evil?' is often, 'Because God did not want robots programmed to love him, and therefore he created man with the potential to sin.'

Malcolm Muggeridge is therefore not unique in suggesting that history is a drama. We talked about his approach to the problem of evil, in the light of this.

Malcolm, this isn't really a theological question, it is intensely practical, because really what the Christian needs to know is this: 'How do I live in a world where there is so much suffering and evil?'

But if you were to eliminate evil, if that were possible, then you would eliminate good – you would eliminate these categories. If you take away evil from each human heart you make people cease to be human beings. Jesus knew who Judas was. But Judas was necessary, he had a part to play.

Malcolm is very fond of recounting an imaginary meeting between two old ladies and William Shakespeare in the eternal shades. He has given different versions of it, but in outline the story is as follows. The two ladies meet Shakespeare, and in conversation they reveal that while they were alive they went to a performance of *King Lear*. They upbraid Shakespeare. How could he let an old man like Lear go through the sufferings and humiliations that he suffered? Shakespeare listens to their complaints, and replies, 'Well, ladies, I could have stepped in and given him a sedative at the end of Act I – but then there would have been no play'.

There are some obvious rejoinders that could be made, in particular to dispute whether the play is worth the suffering – (a point on which one would have liked Lear's opinion). But Malcolm's point is not that history is a beautifully crafted art-object that justifies the suffering that has gone into its making, but that history is a drama rather than a process. Against the theories of evolutionary historians, that history is progressing in a straight line upwards, Malcolm proposes the drama of creation, controlled not by an inner drive forward, but by the creativity of God.

The point arose in conversation when I asked Malcolm about Jesus being alive.

In what sense is the Christ of the Scriptures alive today?

To use a poor example – in the sense that the creativity of his life and purpose is for ever, he is alive in the sense that Macbeth or Lear is alive today.

But the Bible says that Jesus is now at the right hand of God interceding for our sins. If Macbeth was alive in that sense he'd still be walking around Scotland.

It's a poor analogy. But nevertheless, if you take the analogy of the creativity of a great artist and multiply it by a billion, you have something of the idea. Look at a great painting, say, by Velasquez. The faces are alive. They remain alive. Centuries have passed; we don't know who those people were, but they remain alive.

Now that is not an exact equivalent. But it gives you a notion of the sense in which Jesus is still alive. To understand the creativity of God, the nearest parallel we have – which is a million miles away, but is still analogous – is the creativity of man.

But doesn't that make God the author of sin? Shakespeare quite deliberately created Lear as somebody who very foolishly brought about the events of the play.

He revealed the fearful symmetry of it.

But King Lear is a microcosm of the reality of sin in the world. To me what you've said is as if, asked to explain sickness, you pointed at an ulcer and said 'There is the explanation.' But it's an example, not an explanation.

I don't think that is a parallel, David. Sin and suffering exist in the world because without them the drama of our existence cannot point us to the drama of our existence and the destination God has willed for us. We can't fulfil God's purpose in our existence if there is no suffering and no sin. There would be no point in God creating man. He created him with the potentiality for these things because that is the way man fulfils the purpose God has for him.

To me that's been enormously illuminating. I'm not deeply read in theology, and it may seem far-fetched; I don't even know if others have thought the same.

Are you saying either that God brings sin into existence, or that he is particularly pleased that it exists? Because for Shakespeare the evil was essential, it was part of his play. It made it a good play.

No. In that case, the parallel might not be as close as it should be. At the same time, it comes to almost the same thing. Man has to have an experience which will achieve in him that which God wants. And that experience – that drama as I prefer to call it – involves suffering, it involves sin. St. Augustine, you know, in the last resort thanks God for sins.

The 'fortunate fall'?

That's right. I find that is an illumination of something that otherwise I can't see . . .

Malcolm, isn't the goal of creation that evil should finally be done away with?

Yes, when the world no longer belongs to earth and time. But in this period, between time and eternity, evil is inescapable.

Though Wilberforce, for example, seems to have thought there was some point in abolishing slavery . . .

Yes, but that's a cheat, in that there has probably been more slavery in the past few decades than ever before in human history. Slavery's abolished, but there's more slavery than ever. You can't abolish slavery because all slavery is, is one man telling another man what he wants him to do. Similarly with power – if you took away the search for power from the world you would be eliminating human existence. You can't abolish earthly power, either.

But imagine a small street in Manchester, say, where all the houses belong to a wealthy manufacturer who refuses to maintain the properties adequately and charges exorbitant rents – if I were one of those residents I would want to be told rather more than that my suffering was a part of the drama of existence.

Well, of course, in the context of their situation there, they might take some action, they might string him up, and they might feel that they have achieved something.

And indeed they might have solved some of their problems there; but they've only got rid of one man. They haven't altered the overall situation in the world. It's as we were saying, 'He has pulled down the mighty from their seats and exalted the humble and weak' – but if you stop to think about it, then the humble and weak have become mighty . . . so on it goes!

For the Christian, the elimination of suffering and the elimination of evil are not goals to be pursued for their own sake. Of course one seeks to alleviate suffering where that is possible, locally, in part, even though it does not affect the total situation. Mother Teresa in Calcutta works among the destitute and the dying; it is love in action. Of course we must alleviate suffering.

But I must point out too, that the initial caution of the Roman Catholic Church concerning chloroform and such things is fully justified – they haven't been unmitigated blessings by any manner of means. And of course, there is so much that we would never learn if suffering were taken away from the world.

People have been taught to believe that one day something will be available so that there will be no more suffering. But it will never happen. Suffering is an innate part of our existence. And if you eliminate it, or if you manage to make this or that kind of suffering more bearable or even eliminate it altogether – suffering is still there. Men aren't suffering less today because there are drugs and things which ease them of what they endured before. Suffering is subtler than that – suffering is the devil.

How then should the church be acting, in a world that is like that? For example we have the portrait of the early

Church in the New Testament epistles, which clearly has a social role even outside its own membership.

Well, yes, that is true; and the world 'hospital' or 'hospice' reminds us that that is something the Church started. And everything should be done to comfort and help the suffering. But the idea that the fact that their suffering means that there is no God, or that in a little while somebody is going to invent a wonderful pill so that people won't suffer any more and will be happy – utterly wrong. Happiness is a different thing altogether.

There's a parable in the fact that the word originally chosen as the marketing name for Thalidomide was 'Soma'. That was the name of the drug in Aldous Huxley's novel *Brave New World* which was intended to relieve people of all suffering. But in the real world, Soma means babies born without arms. I think God gives us illustrations like that to keep us awake! Otherwise we fall for all this . . . we think, if only we could get rid of competition, if only we could do this that or the other, we'd all be living happily on earth – it isn't true. The whole Soviet regime, too, is a splendid parable. When I think of the great rejoicing in my house when my father told us that the Czar had been replaced, and that there would be no more wars and so on . . .

The drama has to be lived through. Exactly how and why, we will perhaps see in eternity. But we can get a glimpse of it here.

From the question of evil in the cosmos, we turned to discuss the question of individual sin.

What then about the problem of evil in one's own life – the problem of sin?

Something to be deplored!

You see I can imagine this problem of sin causing huge problems in people's minds about whether they are Christians or not. And one thing I can imagine might possibly cause problems for some people who have read your books is that you often talk about 'aspiring' to be a Christian, as though it were something one had to deserve. Can I put it to you – though I'm not trying to place words in your mouth – that being a Christian is as much a matter of fact as being a husband is, and that while one wants to be as good a husband as possible, being a husband isn't a matter of aspiring at all; it's a fact?

I accept that perfectly. I am a Christian solely because I love Christ and wish to follow Christ. But, I am an aspiring Christian – because I know that through my imperfection, weakness, self-indulgence, egotism, all the different attributes of man, I shall do this very inadequately.

What role does repentance play in all that?

A very big one, because as one becomes aware of one's inadequacies and lapses and indeed of their consequences – indeed if you take the example of the most obvious thing, carnality, 'to be carnally-minded is death'; and you realise this is true, you have to continually come to God in repentance.

It's one of the great features of the Christian religion – that we can be forgiven, and that God's capacity to forgive is illimitable. But we go on sinning . . .

What would you say to the belief that it isn't so much what you do*, as the fact that in being a human being you are in a state of sinfulness which is the root problem; and that the* *symptoms, in effect, are only pointers to the fact that the problem is that we are born human beings, and it's that that has to be dealt with.*

But doesn't that amount to almost the same thing? Being a human being means this fallibility.

I'm really thinking back to what we were talking about when we discussed becoming a Christian. I wonder, you see, whether somebody might not interpret what you are saying as meaning that being a Christian is something that you do. It seems to me that in any Christian formulation from any tradition, the initial act, in Catholic mystical literature as much as in extreme Calvinistic Protestant literature, is that first God does something and then in response man does something.

That is right. I would assent to that, that salvation is initiated by an act of God, and that insofar as that is concerned, man's good actions are irrelevant. It is God's grace rather than man's deeds. I think that everything we do on our own is imperfect and inadequate. We need God at every hand and in everything.

What would you say then to somebody who was so overwhelmed by their own inadequacy, so sure that everything they had done was no use, that they were beginning to doubt their own salvation?

I would say first of all that anything anybody does for God is imperfect, because God requires of us a perfection that is unattainable. Even Jesus when he asked to be let off being crucified, even though the whole purpose of his coming was to be crucified, failed to that extent; and thus encouraged all of us who are deeply conscious of our inadequacy in fulfilling God's purpose for us. It has to be so. Have you ever written a sentence

69

with which you are completely satisfied? Neither have I. That is the nature of our life, and we have to recognise it. We are creatures who are in this extraordinary position, that we can understand perfection and yet never achieve it. That is our human situation.

Kitty and I have been saying matins and evensong together for several years now, and I used to think there was something absurd in saying 'We have erred and strayed like lost sheep, we have left undone those things which we ought to have done . . .' – and never to make any improvement, but say it day after day! And then I realised, you see, that even if you say that prayer and go to sleep say at two a.m. and wake up at four a.m., to say it again, still in that short period when you've been asleep you've piled up a few things to confess to.

So you'd see repentance as being central to the Christian experience?

Oh, yes, I would.

CHAPTER FIVE

The Bible

Pliable: 'Come neighbour Christian, tell me now further
what the things are, and how to be enjoyed, whither
we are going?'
Christian: 'I can better conceive of them with my mind,
than speak of them with my tongue: but yet since you
are desirous to know, I will read of them in my Book.'
Pliable: 'And do you think that the words of your book
are certainly true?'
Christian: 'Yes verily, for it was made by him that cannot
lie.'

John Bunyan, *Pilgrim's Progress.*

The truth is that the light which shines in this incredible
book simply cannot be put out.

Malcolm Muggeridge, *The Authority and Relevance of the
Bible in the Modern World* (1976).

Malcolm Muggeridge's interest in the Bible goes back a
long way.

I remember the first time in my life that I asked an awkward question – I've asked a good many since! I asked an elementary school teacher, 'If you have to do things "in order that the prophecy might be fulfilled" – then how is it a prophecy?' But more mature consideration indicates that there is nothing incompatible in it, that something can be a prophecy and yet it's necessary to fulfil it.

Once I was showing off to my grandmother (that's another thing I've been very guilty of all my life) and I pooh-poohed the idea of Daniel in the lions' den, and she turned to me and said: 'If Daniel isn't true then *nothing's* true.' And that made a great impression on me, a very great impression.

He and Kitty use the Authorized Version exclusively, and their affection for it as a great work of literature is similar to their affection for the Book of Common Prayer and Bunyan's *Pilgrim's Progress*. The place they give to the Authorized Version, however, is not only due to its literary qualities.

I was interested in something you wrote about the Authorized Version. You said that though later versions may have translated more accurately, they may not be portraying the truth of what Jesus actually said. I found that fascinating. On the face of it it's completely illogical, that something which is more accurate could be less true. Would you expand on that?

In what way?

Well, for example, would you deal with the obvious cynical response you might encounter, that you're more attached to

King James's men's literary style than to what Jesus actually said?

I wouldn't accept that. I make a distinction, which I think is a very valid one, between meaning and truth. The truth of the Bible is an artistic truth, not a factual truth. The collapse of Christendom in its later stages has come about largely because of people's attempts to relate this Christian statement of the Bible (including of course the Old Testament) to facts and not to truth. Now this is a tremendously important point, because facts and truth are not the same thing. Basic to this is the great debate between Wilberforce the Bishop of Oxford, and Huxley, about Darwinism; Wilberforce lost out completely. He lost because he was prepared to debate and consider the great truths of the incarnation within the terms of reference Huxley was using, that these were 'factual' truths.

It seems to me that the same thing applies to the historicity of the New Testament. I would date the collapse from the time of Schweitzer and others – the 'search for the historical Jesus'. History is so much less real, less true and infinitely less important than the great drama of the incarnation; and I date the collapse of orthodoxy from the time when that sense was lost.

The Authorized Version illustrates this very well. The fact that it's a great work of literature is only a part of it. Inspired works always are great works of literature. The men who translated it were inspired men, and I don't think that anybody who wasn't inspired could have written some of those marvellous passages. You may say to me that that's only an aesthetic judgement, but it's not. Truth itself, in its highest levels, can only be expressed artistically. It's not in our power to express it in any other way.

In the introduction to *Androcles and the Lion,* Bernard Shaw says that Shakespeare's Caesar is completely unreal, because a man such as Shakespeare describes couldn't have done what Caesar did; he couldn't have consolidated a great empire. I disagree with that absolutely. I think Shakespeare's Caesar was more like Caesar than Caesar was! He is the creation of a great artist, conveying the power-seeking in man. Therefore it's a supremely successful portrait; whereas the 'real' Caesar of historians is a very dubious portrayal, rather as a present-day historian might describe Winston Churchill: with a mixture of adulation, sycophancy and all sorts of things.

William Blake was correct when he said that everything about life was a sort of code, and that if you have the key to this code you can see what it's about. For me this is what the Authorized Version is about – it was a moment of enormous importance, bringing together the people who were translating that book – not just getting the words right (sometimes they got the words wrong) – but getting right what the Bible is actually saying.

I was very struck, working on the text of the Authorized Version not long ago, how extremely literal its approach is.

That is true.

I suppose what is really raised here is the whole question of how we can know things. One of the arguments of Strauss, Schweitzer and others – and I agree that they came at the beginning of a catastrophic time for Christianity – was this: 'the facts, as you have received them, are incorrect.' If they were correct in their assumption that we have wrong facts,

74

and on those wrong facts we are basing our assumptions, where do we, for example, find Christ, if we don't find him in the pages of Scripture?

To come at it slightly differently: if facts are not the important thing, how do we find the truth? Because it seems that though facts and truth aren't the same, and Huxley and those others certainly went grievously wrong when they tried to make them so, nevertheless one very good way to get at truth is through the facts.

Jesus, for example, said what he was doing on earth, and if we have a correct record of what his words were, if the facts of that record are true, then we know the truth of what Jesus came to do. If we don't have, or can't trust, the facts, then how do we get at the truth? Is it by intuition?

I do see what you mean. I think the word I would use is Blake's favourite word, 'imaginative'. Insofar as we reach reality at all – the ultimate reality – we reach it through the imagination. Of course we then have to define imagination. Coleridge distinguished between imagination and fancy, the sense and the truth of a thing in factual terms. Blake was a great upholder of this. He refused even to paint from still life or models in case it distorted his view of reality! And his comments are very illuminating.

But Blake did say, 'The eye altering alters all.' And if my eye is altered or your eye is altered, and is therefore different to yours or yours to mine, how can we check on truth? How can we be sure that my idea of truth is the same as yours? Should truth not be absolute and objective?

Yes; but not in the scientific or the factual sense. Christianity has come to grief in its teachers, its priests, and its Churches, wherever there has been precisely this drive to make the imaginative presentation of truth into a factual one.

I'm convinced that the heart of the whole business – and there's nothing on earth I've thought more about than this in the course of my life – is this: that if it is true that Christianity has succumbed to the historical, the scientific 'factual' mind, it will only be reborn in terms of imagination.

The foregoing might tend to give the impression that Malcolm rejects the historicity of the Bible, but that is not the case. In his rejection of any attempt to bind the Bible to mere logic or scientific facts, he does not discard the fact that Jesus walked the earth; to do so would be to undermine the central belief of his faith, the incarnation. His films made in the Holy Land and following the journeys of Paul constantly affirm the historicity of the Biblical account. In *A Twentieth Century Testimony*, he writes of his visit to the wilderness; while drawing out the 'truths' of the wilderness experience as it is described in Scripture, he speculates on the precise area of the wilderness to which Jesus came on a certain date in history.

His companion on his journey to the Middle East was his friend Dr. Alec Vidler, with whom he made the films which form the basis of *Paul, Envoy Extraordinary*. For several years, Malcolm and Kitty attended a weekly Bible study at Dr. Vidler's home in Rye, which is a little way from Robertsbridge where they live. These Bible studies can be sampled in *Read, Mark, Learn*, a series of studies on Mark's Gospel published by Dr. Vidler. It reveals an attractive aspect of the distinguished biblical scholar, who is seen in it as a teacher with a tremendous desire to get people reading and sharing the Bible. The book is not much more than Dr. Vidler's notes for the studies with introductory material, and if one uses it as one's own guide through Mark it is possible to catch something of the flavour of the original meetings. On the cover is a photograph of the group in session, including Malcolm and Kitty; Malcolm especially appears to be hugely enjoying the occasion. The back cover notes comprise Malcolm's brief tribute to Vidler – 'the fifteen of us who gather round him bask in the certainty of his faith and greatly relish his spirited running commentary on the Scriptures – and the equally spirited discussion that follows.'

We talked about this kind of regular group Bible study.

In what ways have you found the regular Bible studies with Dr. Vidler helpful?

Well, Kitty and I had to give them up, because I don't much like driving at night now. I went to them because of him, and I would have liked to have gone on attending, although I must say that for myself I don't find going through the Gospels sentence by sentence the best way to read the Bible. But he's a scholar, and he sees it like that.

What then in your opinion is the most effective way of reading the Bible?

To read it, and as it were to breathe with it. So that as you read it, you're aware of what our Lord has to say – you're listening to him. 'That is the Greek word "so-and-so" ' – I don't particularly want to know that, as I don't know Greek. I'm not criticising Alec. He is a theologian, and he has been a don, and this is his way of expounding the Gospels, and I'm sure it has great

77

utility. But as it happens it's not the way I find most
helpful.

But I did enjoy going to them, firstly because of him,
and also because the people who came were very nice
people. And it was a group of fellow-Christians . . . But
actually what makes the Gospels live to me is when I
see them (particularly the parables) as an expression of
what life is about which is as valid today as it was two
thousand years ago.

*Is this why going to the Holy Land made such an impression
on you?*

Exactly. I went round with Alec following the journeys
of St. Paul, and that was for me an enormous help. It
made me realise what a great man Paul was.

We returned to the theme of knowing Christ. What place,
I asked Malcolm, did the Bible have in this?

*You've mentioned in earlier conversations that one of the
ways the Holy Spirit helps us is in revealing truth to us
through the written word. In what way does the Bible enrich
your experience of Christ?*

Oh, enormously.

*I suppose because the Bible is the revelation of Christ, the
only one we have?*

First of all, yes. Secondly, because our Lord's teaching
– especially the parables – is most fantastic. Putting it
in the most utterly banal way, they must be the most
wonderful stories ever written, in the impact they have
on human beings – after all, they were said two thousand
years ago, and you and I could hardly talk without

referring to them in some way or other. And so that's tremendous.

I must have read the New Testament right through, I don't know how many times. When we get to the end Kitty and I go back to the beginning. And each time it seems to be more enriching. The extraordinary sagacity and shrewdness of our Lord about the world! A very good example is his comment that if you look after a woman with intent to lust after her, you've committed adultery. That's really an observation that in the ordinary way, only a sinner could make! But he knew all the things like that . . .

He had this extraordinary understanding of human beings. Not of course that he had acquired a sinful nature by becoming a man without being aware of sensuality, just as he couldn't have become a man without experiencing pain. Otherwise the crucifixion was nothing. And we couldn't have had that marvellous incident where he says 'Please let me off' – a marvellous touch!

Considering Malcolm's constant reference to the New Testament and the Gospels, and his fascination with the person and earthly life of Jesus, I wondered how important he thought the Old Testament, and what unity he saw between the two.

You have the Old Testament which tells you all the various expectations which were entertained in preparation for Christ's appearance on earth. The New Testament without the old would be considerably hampered. I see nothing incompatible between the Testaments. The Gospel writers make it quite clear that while Christ was on earth he was quite deliberately fulfilling the prophecies of the Old Testament.

What relationship do you find between the revelation of God in Christ, and the revelation of God in the Bible? Do you place them in any sort of order of priority?

Through the New Testament alone do we know Christ. We know what he said he was, what he did, and so on. It is the drama of his life on earth, and therefore it is the only source of knowledge we have; and in that sense it is unique.

And I must say that the more I read the New Testament – and I read it quite a lot – the more I'm struck by what a literary feat it is. How clearly the character of this man stands out! And how enormously shrewd – quite apart from any other characteristics – are the things he is saying; how realistic, how complete his understanding of our life. His use of parables . . . things like that. So far as knowing Christ is concerned, the Bible tells us what happened when Christ came to earth.

CHAPTER SIX

Fellowship and the Church

The Spirit of Christ can set men free and enable them to become their true selves without requiring their dependence on any particular religious organisation.

Alec Vidler, 'Religion and the National Church', in *Soundings* (1962).

I know perfectly well that, however much I may long for it to be otherwise, the bell does not ring for me. Nor is there a place for me at the altar rail where they kneel to receive the Body of Christ. I should be an outsider there, too.

Malcolm Muggeridge, *Something Beautiful for God* (1971).

Worship . . . it's one of the things that I have missed most as a Christian. Probably through my own fault.

Malcolm Muggeridge in conversation, 1982.

When I first talked with Malcolm Muggeridge about his discipleship, the subject I was most curious about was his

81

attitude to Church fellowship. It seemed to be the only major gap in his Christian experience, the only thing that one never found him writing about positively. The faults of the institutional Church are pointed out everywhere in his books. *Something Beautiful for God* has Malcolm's inability to join the Church so much as a subsidiary theme that a large part of his portrait of Mother Teresa is achieved by his account of her discussions and correspondence with him on the subject.

Malcolm agreed that the subject was one which he had not written very much about, and that in a book on discipleship it was obviously important. We touched on the subject several times in other contexts: for example, when talking about the evangelical experience of conversion, he spoke of his son, who attends a Brethren Church. Malcolm has a very high regard for the Brethren.

They're marvellous people. I have a great love and respect for them. My son goes to a Brethren Church – they built a little meeting house where he lives. It means that in these troubled times they have a little group of people there who help each other.

The subject of church fellowship arose again when we talked, as we often did, about Mother Teresa.

She has no plans. She won't even allow people to put money in trust for her, because she says 'I only want to live with the poorest of the poor; they have no security, and I want no security.'

But she is much more structured than you in some ways – she wanted you to join the church, for example.

She did, because she has certain views of the Catholic

Church, and that to her was of tremendous importance, and she was kind enough to want me to be in it. And . . . we had talks about it, and so on . . .

But it is also true that even she has said to me, 'I see that God can be served in a great variety of ways', and was kind enough to say that I am serving God.

In other words, even on that she doesn't make it an ultimate condition of anything.

It was late in 1982 when we sat down to talk specifically about the fellowship of the Church. We talked about worship.

As I see it, it's one of the things that I have most missed as a Christian, and yet I think more and more that it's absolutely essential.

You're talking here about corporate worship rather than individual worship?

Yes, I'm talking about meeting with fellow Christians, praising God, saying prayers together. Being together enclosed for a while, more in eternity than in time. It makes a little clearing.

That is why I believe worship should belong to the mystery, rather than become what so many people are trying to make it, an extension of everyday life. For example, the idea that if you have people twanging guitars in everyday life, you must have people twanging guitars in church.

I live in the country in a village with a beautiful old church; but I never go there, though I quite like the vicar. I simply don't have that sense of partaking of the mystery when I go there. This may be morbid, but so many Churches seem to have about them the smell of decay. In some cases it's in the very fabric, which needs attention – I don't know, the whole thing seems a bit shabby. And so saying matins and evensong with my wife which I do every day, and a bit more on Sunday, takes me more into the realm of worship than going to Church does.

We had been talking about the fact that the Bible makes certain claims on our lives, that the Christian life has an element of obedience.

Do you feel that there's a biblical commandment here, that one should attend worship? When you say that you have missed worship, do you feel that you have missed something that you ought to have had – something which it was your obligation as a Christian to have had?

Very much so . . .

Why do you say that?

Well, I feel it would have kept me on a more . . . I mean it would have kept me more closely related to what I want to be related to . . . After all, we do have to live in the world, we do have to earn our living, we're subject to all the temptations of the world (the one I've had most difficulty with is carnality, simply because that's the indulgence I've found hardest to cope with). And if you don't have worship, if you don't reach God along with a lot of other people, it would be like saying that you go on a pilgrimage, but you go by yourself. Whereas it's the essence of pilgrimage that you go with other travellers. Going back to my Bunyan

man, he always had a few other people with him, and
sometimes quite a crowd . . .

I'll tell you another thing which is an interesting aspect
of television, which is one seldom mentioned, but it's
the only one I would point to to say that in that respect
at least television truly enriched my life. And that is
this, that if you claim yourself a Christian on television
then you become known at any rate as somebody who
is an aspiring Christian. You find, of course, that people
recognise you, and quite often people come up to you
and say, 'I too love the Lord', or something like that.
Sometimes until you get used to it you might
misunderstand it; you're leaving a restaurant and the
waiter comes padding after you and you think, 'I
haven't given him enough of a tip' or something, and
he says 'I just wanted to shake your hand; I believe in
the same Person'.

That's very refreshing. And the interesting thing is that
they're a whole variety of people, but you'd never dream
of saying, 'Excuse me, but what denomination do you
belong to?' They're my brothers and sisters. Or you
might – something happened to me the other day – I
turned the corner and there was an enormous black
man, and smiles broke out all over his face and we
clasped hands – well, that is the Christian fellowship;
which I think is enormously valuable, and which I think
worship ought to provide.

My eldest son, who is in the Brethren, has the most
perfect relationship with worship, and not even just in
theoretical terms, but in practical; they help each other.
His little boy, his youngest little boy, was thought to
have meningitis – fortunately it wasn't, but things

seemed very black. He had to be rushed to hospital.
Well, the Brethren all came round – one of the doctors
belonged to the Church and made a special effort,
etcetera, etcetera. I found that very beautiful; and
worship is the same sort of thing. And I've missed it.
I've missed it. Probably through my own fault.

*May it not be partly because of where you live? I think the
meeting of the Church in worship is merely the local evidence
of something which is a reality at a whole community level
– and you live in a fairly remote spot, where there may not
be all that many Christians around.*

I wish that were true, but it was the same when I was
living in Albany in central London – St. James' Church
was opposite and I practically never went into it, or St.
Paul's or anywhere – simply because I was out of tune
with the Anglican Church . . .

Fellowship, experiencing together the wonderful sense
of brotherliness between those who love our Lord, and
the common feeling of joy to be a creature of his creation
related to these wonderful truths – that's what you miss
if you don't find worship.

*How would you advise somebody who has just become a
Christian, or who hasn't been a Christian for very long?*

I would say, 'Find fellow-worshippers.' I wouldn't
necessarily say 'Go to your local Church,' because I
wouldn't be automatically hopeful that it would be
helpful. But if you worship with others who love the
Lord, it will tremendously enhance your faith, and
strengthen you when you feel weakened. Most certainly
that would be my advice.

Funnily enough, the only time that Kitty and I were

completely content with worship, was when I had to do some work in the South of France, and we stayed in a little place in the hills behind Nice. There was an old church in the village, and there was a very delightful elderly priest who hadn't got involved in any of the present debates. And we went to Mass every single morning! We didn't partake, but we got to know the service – of course he did the classic Mass, but it was in French not Latin, and I got to know it well. And there would usually be one or two peasant women there, dressed in black, whose joints creaked when they kneeled down; joyful people to be with. And they with ourselves – three Protestants! – were the only congregation.

And I've never felt so happy in worship, or so looked forward to worshipping, as there.

It was at this point in our conversation that Malcolm asked me to switch my tape recorder off, and then told me what several weeks later was to become a major news story – that he and Kitty were candidates to be received into the Roman Catholic Church.

Malcolm is writing his own book about his conversion to Catholicism, and we agreed together that he would not deal with the subject in our conversations. He was very happy to talk about it informally, however, and once having broken the news found it hard to resist coming back to the subject with obvious pleasure.

At the end of the project, when this book was almost ready to go to press and the news of Malcolm and Kitty's reception into the Catholic Church was no longer a main story in the newspapers, I visited Malcolm to clear up a few final matters. I asked him if he would mind if I hazarded my own guesses at the factors which had influenced him. He agreed readily.

When I look back at our conversations, and read your books, I would think that one factor – though probably not the strongest – was the stand of the Roman Catholic Church on certain ethical issues about which you feel strongly.

Yes, abortion, and so on. Very important. It's a big factor because one can say 'This is a losing battle, and I want to be with the side that's right, openly and publicly.' Very important, though as you say it could not be the decisive factor.

Another thing which I find very striking about the Roman Catholic Church is that for so much of western history, it was Christendom; although never perfect because of schism and then the Reformation, nevertheless it does have a historical unity which Protestantism, with its different origins, does not have. Did the concept of the unity of Christendom as displayed in the Catholic Church appeal to you? Especially in view of your opinions on the difference between earthly and spiritual power.

Yes. With all its ups and downs . . .

You have been very rude about the Catholic Church in the past . . . !

Yes, and I could well be so again! But with all its blemishes, and I would never hide them, it has that extraordinary continuity from the walk to Emmaus onwards . . . it is a most extraordinary thing.

How important was it for you that the Church speak with a united voice on the ethical issues? Protestantism is highly divided.

That appealed to me too, though it was a negative point – Catholicism is less divided than Protestantism.

The conversation was brief, and more to satisfy my curiosity than for Malcolm to fully explain his reasons for joining the Church. That must wait for the publication of his own account. It may well be his most significant book.

I have been asked by Protestant friends what my reaction was when I heard Malcolm's news. For what it is worth, I can only place on record the tremendous pleasure one feels that Malcolm, for so long an outsider at the feasts of God, is now inside the gates. The Church of Christ is the most precious gift God has given to twentieth-century mankind. Whatever the reasons for it (and some of them were extremely persuasive), Malcolm's alienation from the fellowship throughout his long life has always been something which has made many of his fellow-Christians very sad for him. To hear him announce that he and Kitty were to be received into the fellowship, and to share his joy, was a great privilege. In this instance, the brand of Church is quite immaterial.

CHAPTER SEVEN

Earthly Powers

The work of a Beethoven, and the work of a charwoman,
become spiritual on precisely the same condition, that
of being offered to God, of being done humbly 'as to
the Lord'.

C. S. Lewis, *Transposition and Other Essays.*

There is a well-known story of a Hollywood magnate
who, when his staff brought him a scenario of H. G.
Wells's Outline of History, asked them if they couldn't
work in a love interest. Much criticism has been levelled
at this excellent man . . . He was on the right track,
even if he hadn't gone very far along it.

Hugh Kingsmill, *Lloyd George.*

My time in Moscow made me realise the diffcrence
between Utopias and Heaven, and understand the
greater appeal of the latter. A Utopia is simply a place
where a different set of people are important, whereas
in Heaven everyone is important. Thus mankind has,
very creditably, for the most part plumped for heaven.
It has been rightly suspicious of Utopias, and only

91

allowed Utopias to have their innings when things got very bad indeed.

Malcolm Muggeridge, writing in 'Time and Tide', 1934.

The relationship between Malcolm and Kitty Muggeridge and Beatrice and Sidney Webb was a precarious one when the Webbs were alive; after many years, the edge of Malcolm's sardonic view of these two founding-figures of modern socialism is not blunted. The final pages of his second volume of autobiography – *The Infernal Grove* – in which he describes the installation of the Webb's ashes in Westminster Abbey are bitingly funny.

Beatrice Webb was Kitty's aunt, and the two volumes of *Chronicles of Wasted Time* give numerous domestic glimpses of the Webbs in and out of public view. They figure largely in Malcolm's disillusionment with the Soviet Union, where he went hoping to find a viable society of the future. The Soviet society which defeated those hopes idolised the Webbs.

For Malcolm, the early socialists were pursuing the goal of human happiness, but their basis for hope was quite wrong. We talked about the ethical teachings of some early Labour leaders.

Do you feel then that there is a gap between ethics and Christianity, that you can have one without the other? It is certainly implied in your books when you talk about socialism.

Yes, I do very much think so.

Do you think that the reason for that shortfall is because human beings are incapable of achieving satisfactory ethical standards; or would you say that they can achieve them but

*that's not the direction to go? What I mean is, do you think
that socialism is a workable idea that has not worked, but
could be made to work?*

No. I would say that by its nature it is bound to fail.

Why?

Because it is materialistic. Because it is founded on the
assumption that men can create a perfect society
themselves. And they can't.

*Is there a possibility at all that a society based on socialist
principles could, if not create a perfect society, at least
adequately care for its sick, adequately care for its elderly,
have a national health service that doesn't end up dispensing
however many tranquillisers it is every day . . .?*

No.

*Have we let Aneurin Bevan down? Or did he start out with
the wrong idea?*

I don't think we let him down. Because Nye himself –
I knew him quite well, and liked him – was dissatisfied
with the whole thing when he died. I met him shortly
before then, and he said that the only correct policy for
us would be to proclaim that we must lower our
standards of living in order to help all these people, the
starving and so on.

*Did the Labour Party see itself at that time as putting into
force, more effectively than the Church, Jesus's teachings?*

That was very much so. Jesus was a good man, they
said, and naturally therefore the establishment killed
him. That was the argument.

How would you attack that position?

93

It completely ignored the incarnation. It argued that Jesus might have had fantasies about being the prophesied messiah, but his ethics were estimable and his followers grossly betrayed him by establishing a Church and a hierarchy which, to my father's friends, were very far from being related to the Gospels.

I think that was the accepted view among those people. They were quite a little group, you see, they were all socialists in the context of a London suburb. They met and talked a lot about these things, and I used to listen avidly.

Was there much disillusionment?

Yes, some people left. Douglas Hyde, for example, who wrote a book called *I believed,* reverted to Catholicism. He was the Foreign Editor of the Daily Worker, and I knew him quite well.

I asked Malcolm about the social conscience of the Labour Party. Hadn't that been a strong element in its history?

Do you find in any of these people – the Webbs, HG Wells, etc. – any feeling that the meek might inherit the earth?

Well yes. Of course the meek, the poor, are the people who understand life best. And of course they might go under, but they have a better chance of understanding it, because wealth and pride and lechery and all the things which are the birthright of the rich are the most destructive things.

At what point then did the power quest take over from the 'meek shall inherit the earth' quest?

You mean in the case of the Webbs?

94

All right.

When they persuaded themselves that power can make people good. That is the basic fallacy. It only makes them bad. History is full of examples. Hitler, Mussolini, they must have thought that through power they were creating happier circumstances.

Is this the 'green stick' which Tolstoy once believed existed, on which were carved words that would make men good?

Yes. One got the thing from Tolstoy to a great extent, and Dostoievsky who was more perceptive, but in a sense they were saying the same thing.

So – you are saying categorically that morality has to be validated by Christianity, that morals without Christianity are fundamentally inadequate.

For we Western people.

In what sense do you mean that?

I mean that we have grown up in a civilisation that is based on the Christian revelation. All our insights and great art and mores are deeply stamped by this. Therefore for us Christianity is both the definition and means of virtue.

Look at the way people have tried. The Christian Socialist movement, with which of course I've had dealings in my day, is really a complete flop. Donald Soper said to me once, 'The Labour Party gave Christianity its legs.' I said, 'Donald, when I think where those legs have carried it!' Donald is a good man, but I believe the movement has failed.

I recently saw, however, a television play – Boys from the Blackstuff *– which did demonstrate something of what it*

*is like to live in a city with 20% unemployment, where every
fifth person you meet is unemployed; and it does seem as
though, when you see a programme like that, there is no
problem in life more important than dealing with
unemployment.*

It's very interesting you should say that, because you see
when I was on the Manchester Guardian in 1930–1932,
that was the period of the Great Depression. Some of
those towns in Lancashire had 60% unemployment. I
felt exactly as you do. And then I thought, the only
alternative is the Soviet System. That was why Kitty
and I decided we would go to the USSR and live the
rest of our lives there. And it was there that I learned
that the whole idea that you can, through power,
provide human beings with a loving and brotherly and
prosperous and contented environment and state of
mind – is completely a fallacy. They've created a life
that is infinitely more hellish for the individuals in it
than the most appalling breakdown of society. But I
know your feelings, and I had exactly your feelings,
and the situation was possibly worse, there was poorer
welfare. Unemployment – especially in Lancashire –
was extremely high. And there were people hanging
around the streets. So we knew all about that.

I felt (and wrote) then that it was the breakdown of the
Capitalist system, and that's true, the Capitalist system
had broken down. But God knows, so has the Marxist
one. When you think of the history of the last thirty or
forty years, and the mad imperialistic system they have
now adopted, running over other countries and so
on . . .

I was in Germany recently. I realised that one place I

wanted to visit was in East Germany, and I hadn't got a
visa. And when I looked at the map, quite near from where
I was staying there was a wavy line printed right down the
map: and it was very odd to think, that is the Curtain.

That's the Curtain. Absolutely. The one thing common
to all socialist regimes is a border guarded by soldiers,
dogs, landmines, tanks – you might like to think it's to
stop people from coming in! But it's to stop people
getting out. Do you know, before they built the wall,
nine million Germans moved westward. The other day
in Cuba some Latin American country said it was
prepared to issue visas. Ten thousand people gathered
demanding these visas. One thing every Communist
state has is that everyone wants to get out of it.

But the Capitalist system doesn't offer anything better
– except for people like you and me. It's better for us.
But it's moving in the same direction without being
aware of it.

So you wouldn't say, better a dead capitalist than a live
socialist?

Well I wouldn't say that or the other way round. The
capitalist system doesn't provide an alternative, to make
people contented. And it never will.

What do you think the answer is? Sanctified capitalism, or
sanctified socialism?

Well, neither: if I were prophesying I would say there
will be a general breakdown in both. The communist
system has broken down, it is only its ruthless power
that keeps it going; and of course the capitalist system
is bust. There will be the twentieth century equivalent
of the dark ages. I have no expectation that the capitalist

system will pull itself together because there's nothi
to pull together. It's not in ruins because it doesn't
exist.

Whatever the Christian basis of Western society was, is it
now dissipated too far to pull it back together?

In terms of power, yes. But then you see God doesn't
leave us like that, and you see Solzhenitszen popping
up in that unexpected place, and saying 'I never knew
what freedom was until I lost it, and came to this place;
now I know it.' To me that is simply marvellous. And
of course I believe him when he says that probably at
least a third of the population would cordially agree with
him. There are probably many more Christians in the
USSR than in America now.

When I was in Germany I went to visit Beethoven's
birthplace in Bonn. Afterwards I visited the Schloss Bruhl,
a few kilometres away. I was struck by the contrast between
the humbleness of Beethoven's birthplace and the baroque
splendour of the Schloss. The Archbishop's children were
born in that palace, and who has ever heard of the
Archbishop? But Beethoven . . .

That's a good image of the fantasy of success and power
and money.

Among my books is one that Malcolm gave me. It is a proof
copy of the published diaries of Beatrice Webb, copiously
annotated in the black fibre-tip with which Malcolm tends
to mutilate his books (Book-lovers tend to divide into the
collectors and the readers. Malcolm reads). The passages
he has chosen to underline reflect his ambivalent attitude
to Mrs. Webb; to have marked the sentences he has done
indicates a sympathetic, if rigorous, reading of the diaries.

98

One poignant comment he has drawn a black line under is this: 'If I gain personal power, shall I walk humbly with my God?' Malcolm has underlined it without comment.

The theme of earthly powers was a recurring element in our conversations. Malcolm has said many times that he believes that Christendom as we have known it is coming to an end. In a recent published interview he said,

'I think you who are young will live to see the collapse of institutions like the Anglican Church. I would say that what's called Christendom is now at an end . . . the power-structure that's built on the Gospels – it's over. It's been 2,000 years of remarkable history, but it's over.

Christ can survive. What he said doesn't stand or fall by Christendom. We've got a marvellous example of that in that one of the places where the marvellous rebirth of the Christian faith is most marked is in the labour camps of the USSR – the most unlikely place in the world . . . and I can see why.

If you have a vocation to be a minister you can do anything in the world that appeals to you because you can do it for and with Christ. You are a representative of Christ in the world and you help people to understand what it's all about. Marvellous. And a marvellous time for it.'

I asked Malcolm about his views of the ultimate future of the world.

What about the second coming? Jesus promised his disciples he would return.

Well, it's prophesied.

Do you think of it as a visible historic event, that will actually take place, like the first coming?

I don't know; because I don't think we're able to know that.

So you are not too worried that your expectations of dying in the fairly near future might be thwarted by something dramatic happening?

It's conceivable. But I don't think it probable. I think, again, one has to say 'Thy will be done.' It has been specifically said, there will be a second coming, that the incarnation was not just one thing.

Some people have suggested that the 'second coming' will be merely a great revival of religion.

I would be very surprised if that were the case. I'm rather suspicious of great revivals of religion. In the past some of them have turned out to be fraudulent.

You are looking rather, so far as one can see, for something of a historic nature, an event?

With God all things are possible . . . it would be presumptuous to say, that will be or this will be. All things are possible with God. Even rich men can be good . . .

CHAPTER EIGHT

The Love of God

He threatens terrible things if we will not be happy.

Jeremy Taylor

Talking to Malcolm Muggeridge meant that conversation often turned to God's love. It is a theme he loves to discuss, and which he cannot keep long away from. It arose, for example, when we had been talking about God's guidance, a subject we talked about often. I have included this conversation almost unedited, because it illustrates for me that Malcolm's faith is robust enough to face what might seem hard questions if one gave no place to the love of God.

One problem area in this whole thing about guidance, it seems to me, is that if all the available options were equally good, in the sense of morally good, then there wouldn't be a problem; but it seems to me that where one might very well pray for guidance is where one thinks that there is a real possibility that one might fall into sin – one might do something which was not only contrary to God's purposes but also to his character.

101

Mmm – of course it is possible. But also the other way round. By pondering and thinking 'Is this what I must do – or that?', one might do the wrong thing – you see?

I'm very fond of Bunyan. The whole imagery of the *Pilgrim's Progress* touches my heart more than I can tell you. I love it as a book. It's brilliant and in a way funny, and I believe it's profoundly correct. There's a passage I often say to myself where he's walking along I forget with whom, and the road begins to climb steeply, and whoever is with him says 'Wouldn't it be rather nice if we took a rendezvous without climbing up?' The conclusion is, 'No; the Way is the Way, and there is an end.' In other words we can almost sleepwalk it. If we are in the Way we shall know it is the Way, if we are in the right relationship to God. It is only the Way that matters. Nothing else matters at all.

But the Lord's prayer is actually very specific, isn't it. I mean it does include the prayer, deliver us from evil.

Yes it does, and one doesn't want to be led into temptation either. It's a very beautiful prayer and is full of tender considerations for human beings. One of the most marvellous things is that as far as material things are concerned it just limits itself to 'Give us this day our daily bread' – and not going into the question of tomorrow or yesterday.

What would you say then, to the person who comes to you racked by guilt, and in the grip of some sin that they – let's say for the sake of example somebody who is having an extramarital affair which they just cannot get out of because there has been a dependency established between the man and his mistress – perhaps the ramifications are too complicated for him to simply be able to turn his back.

The person may simply say, 'Well if you say, simply pray "Thy will be done" and if we say "Simply look for the Way and try to follow it" – well, that sounds awfully easy but in fact practically it's very difficult, and I want to know exactly what I do; here am I, my wife doesn't know anything about it but I've actually got this mistress up in Edinburgh or Glasgow or York or whatever, and I go up every three weeks supposedly on business, and I've got this relationship now; I pay part of her rent; you know, there are a whole lot of practical things involved, and yet I don't know exactly what practical thing I must do to solve it.' And that person might ask you how to find out from God what to do next. 'It's all very well to say "Wait on God," but it's not that easy in my situation,' they might say.

Well, I agree, I see exactly the force of what you say; but I still think that the only way that I would ever advise anybody in that situation would be to put aside all the considerations you've mentioned and wait on God and, in the light of that, proceed.

Would you go so far as to say that having done that, in the light of that, you would expect God to tell you how to proceed?

Well – yes – I can say that. But to me it wouldn't seem like that. To me it would seem to be in the logic of the situation. Let me tell you another thing that is deeply rooted in everything I feel about and have to say about this subject. The sentence I would use is simply the one I have used before; this I consider to be most important: 'Life is a drama, not a process.' Now you've got to look at our lives in that way, say as though it were a Shakespearean play. You could have a Shakespearean play about the very situation you're describing. If the

103

drama was written by Shakespeare, someone who
understood by his genius what it was really about, as
distinct from what it would seem to be about in X, Y
or Z's eyes, the great drama has its own denoument.
Lear had to divide his kingdom, be out in the world
storm, learn at last through that experience that all his
hopes and fears and regrets were nothing; and we have
that marvellous speech at the end: We two will away to
prison – and laugh at the world – 'and take upon's the
mystery of things as if we were God's spies.'

In other words if you see man's situation not as an 'either-
or' situation but as a drama, and like all dramas it has
its built-in, correct ending, and that through waiting
on God and through detaching himself from his personal
interest or personal appetites, he will find out what is
the correct denouement, then all will be well.

*I take the point. Now may I come from another direction?
I think that the person coming to you in the situation I have
described would be asking, not so much 'Is God in control
of all these things? Does God have a purpose? Is there a
plot to his crazy drama?' What they will be wanting
basically to know is, 'Does God care?' And at that point
he might well be put off if you say that God isn't interested
in the details of daily life.*

Perhaps it's an unfortunate choice of words; but there
might be a difficulty in the other direction if you give
people the impression that if they ask God properly, he
will give them their marching orders.

*I'm suggesting that one can approach God and ask, I'm not
saying we can demand anything.*

In a way – yes. People can, and if that's the way they
want to do it, they can live that way, but for me, I

wouldn't ask God. I would try so to attune myself to
God that I would know how the drama should work
out. There's a right way for it to work out, and I would
know. I would be led along from one thing to another,
precisely because that's what the drama requires.

*Many people are buffeted along, aren't they? The
unemployed person for example who doesn't bother to get
up in the morning because there's nothing to do – it's very
hard for someone who is being pushed around by life to
change into a situation where –*

Oh yes, but we all are pushed around by life at times,
and it's only a matter of degree. And the unemployed
man whose life has been so messed up because there's
no work for him can find himself, and find work, by
realising that it's not a matter of life and death whether
you have a paid job, but that any given moment
anywhere in the universe there are things that can be
done that are loving and useful. So let's get at them.

*What about the image of the sparrows? 'Two sparrows sold
for a farthing' – 'every hair of your head is numbered' . . .*

I love that image. It's perfectly true that God cares
utterly for his creation, and can't see a sparrow fall to
the ground without concern; and at the same time he
tells us to take no thought for the morrow, and that we
are looked after, and that if we are with him and with
him through his son, who became a man in order to
help us; even things like being employed or
unemployed, sick or well, sharpwitted or foolish, don't
have the importance people think they have. I think for
instance that when people are writing about our time,
one of the things that will convince them that we were
on the wrong tack is psychiatry. The idea that by

investigating our minds and putting questions to us they can help us, relate us to life. Being related to life is nothing. Being related to God is everything.

I don't put this out as the only way. But it is the way that has appealed to me. And every time I have been tormented as to whether I am going to do this or do that, I've always felt that it's an unworthy attitude.

I do see exactly what you mean. The unemployed man, the man with his mistress, these people do have specific problems before them. But those problems are only significant to the degree that they reach beyond those problems into the whole essence of their existence; then they can deal with them.

I think I might be tempted to feel somewhat short-changed in that situation. I might think, 'Well, he's made every snowflake different – and he's not telling me where my next move is coming from! I might feel that concern over the creation had rather overtaken concern for the individual.

Yes, that's a perfectly understandable statement. But I think the way to live – none of us can do it wholly – the way to life is to take no thought for anything, but what God wants, and what is the destiny of life and therefore the destiny in which we, to an infinitesimal degree, participate.

CHAPTER NINE

Dying

Many people will have been saddened to learn of the sudden death of Malcolm Muggeridge at the age of 150.

Auberon Waugh, 1960.

For several years, Malcolm Muggeridge has spoken openly, eloquently and often about his approaching death. He has not simply enjoyed the role of an old man raising an eyebrow at the follies of the young; he enjoys old age for its own sake, and one of the reasons is that it means his death is close at hand.

First acquaintance with Malcolm's openness on the subject can be disconcerting, even if one considers oneself free from the twentieth-century obsession with the preservation of life at all costs (providing, these days, one is neither very young – say an unwanted foetus – or very old, and a prospective customer for a euthanasia kit). It might be said that he has shot his bolt too soon; in 1980 he told a television chat show host that he was looking forward to death, and he has repeated it many times since. When you meet him, he is remarkably healthy, showing relatively few of the handicaps of old age, and certainly not at all resembling somebody who has been announcing his imminent death for the past few years.

But talking to him at any length one realises how integral his view of death is to his whole view of life. The end of being a stranger in a strange land; the end of the flesh, which has snared him throughout life and will go on snaring him until the end of it; the passing of earthly powers and the ushering in of heavenly realities – in a sense he has always been talking about death, even when he was young. We mistake him if we interpret his talk of death as the announcement of an end. It is for him a beginning, a new adventure.

Because much of our conversation was to do with the day-to-day experiences of Christianity, we did not talk much about dying. There are not many extended discussions on the tapes of our talks together. But it is an ever-present backdrop to the whole of his understanding of life. It enhances it.

'Like a glorious day, that you see fading just before the night comes and then the dawn – and you feel a heightened sense of enjoyment, a desire to experience it to the full. It is a bitter-sweet moment, because it is fading and you want to know as much of it as possible.'

My impression of Malcolm's view of dying is not therefore of a sustained discussion; we did not have one. My impression is instead one of references and allusions cropping up in every discussion we had: like the evening sun flooding through the window of the Ark, catching us in a late glow, illuminating, but not needing much comment.

I would like to close this record of our conversations with a quotation from Malcolm; not about dying, but living.

'So far as we have now gone, Christianity is the ultimate truth about life, and we try to follow it; and if God were kind enough to think that I was following it a bit carefully or adequately by my present way of life I would of course be overjoyed; but I leave that judgement in his hands.'

Postscript

There is the Way, and the journey's end.

Thomas Traherne, *The Way to Blessedness.*

'What! No Mount Sion? Did we not see the Delectable Mountains from the Gate of the City? Also, are we not now to walk by faith? Let us go on,' said Hopeful, 'lest the man with the whips overtakes us again.'

John Bunyan, *Pilgrim's Progress.*

Malcolm Muggeridge continues to work every day: there are several projects he is completing, and answering letters takes a lot of time. His working day follows a disciplined pattern, but is liable to frequent interruption.

Claiming the privileges of old age, he rarely ventures far from home; 'Anyone who wants me for anything can come here.' He was recently lured to London, by a group of fellow-journalists who had organised a dinner to celebrate his eightieth birthday – 'It would have rather cast a blight on it if I hadn't turned up.' But usually people make the journey down to Robertsbridge. His children come often, with their children, and so do Fleet Street colleagues, whose news is devoured with gusto. 'I feel rather like a retired whore,' he remarked to one journalist. 'I like to see what the new girls in the whorehouse are getting up to.' When I went to see him shortly before completing his book, the newspapers were beginning to probe the problems of independent television's new breakfast programmes – a complicated story which only became front-page news a week or so later. Malcolm was well-informed on the subject. Somebody at the centre of the disputes had been down to see him the day before and had brought him up to date.

Into this crowded programme Malcolm inserted several meetings with me. They were spread over a year because arrangements often had to be revised owing to some fresh demand on his time. When he and Kitty were received into the Catholic Church, his morning postbag, always large, increased dramatically. Telephoning on one occasion to postpone a planned visit, he explained 'Of course one can't hope to answer every single letter – but even reading them all is such a wonderfully emotional experience.' In between visits to Robertsbridge, I reread Muggeridge's books and other writings.

After a year largely focussed on Malcolm Muggeridge, I asked myself as I completed this book in the weeks following Easter 1983, what had I discovered through my encounter with him? I had set out with few preconceptions beyond a liking for his work and an admiration for his public stance as a Christian on issues that I believed in. I had introduced myself to him by explaining that I was an evangelical Christian; he made it clear from the beginning that though he had a great love and respect for the evangelical tradition, he did not consider himself an evangelical. Halfway through the project, he entered the Roman Catholic Church after a lifetime as a nominal Anglican. It might seem that after my twelve months of Muggeridge, the conundrum remains as perplexing as ever.

But though it would be foolish to claim that a handful of conversations and a reading of his books have enabled me to exhaustively analyse Muggeridge (a futile enterprise even if one took a decade about it), my encounter with him has had several distinct and helpful results in my own life and my own understanding of Christianity.

My initial interest in his Christianity had been prompted by the fact that he seemed to have allowed a great number of his writings to remain in print, which one might have thought to have been rendered obsolete by later pieces. Why had he allowed the agnostic speculations of parts of *Jesus Rediscovered* to stand, when in more recent statements he has spoken with certainty and confidence? Why should he have left in print a pronouncement to the effect that he didn't know whether he was a Christian or not? If Muggeridge was a Christian, then what sort of a Christian was he, to put his name to such things?

I found several different answers as I talked with him. The first was a very practical one. He has produced such an enormous quantity of writing over the years that it is no longer possible to draw a linear path of development through it. Certainly one can, as I have done in the chapter headings in this book, juxtapose quotations taken from different periods, and so project a trend. But one is liable to be confounded by the fact that a quotation which contradicts that trend is always likely to turn up, like a fossil appearing in the wrong stratum of rock to destroy the theories of geologists.

The reason is not difficult to find. Like most writers who have written prolifically, Muggeridge frequently falls back on re-using old material. Certain jokes, examples, anecdotes and quotations reappear throughout his writings. In conversation he uses a similar device; like the ancient Homeric bards, he will periodically slip into a well-worn topic of conversation (be it Stalin's deathbed, or William Blake on the imaginative eye, or Shakespeare's King Lear). This allows him to prepare his next verbal onslaught ahead of time, while his mind is not too occupied with what he is saying. In the same way, the bards filled up whole lines celebrating 'Aurora's rosy fingers caressing the wine-dark sea', while they got their next epic simile ready for delivery.

If you point this out to him he will smile disarmingly. 'When you get to my age,' he explains, 'you've said more or less everything you have to say on most subjects.' And in his prolific output it is only to be expected that effective material will be used more than once. To a casual reader it can appear as if all stages of Muggeridge's development are simultaneously present in his writing at a particular time.

It might be added that something that gives him the greatest pleasure is to be told that particular things he has written have helped somebody or have influenced them towards Christianity. Consequently he is reluctant to lose material which he knows has been helpful in that way. Many of the pieces in *Jesus Rediscovered*, he readily admits, are now dated and do not reflect precisely how he sees things now. But the collection as a whole has been of help and encouragement to so many people that he is unwilling to change it.

But I think there is another reason for the fact that Muggeridge is content to leave in print statements which might seem to contradict his present views. It is this. For Malcolm, faith and the Christian life are a process of becoming, a road which leads to completeness but has not yet arrived there. If Auberon Waugh's pleasant joke is proved true and Muggeridge does live to be 150 years old, it will still be a fact – according to Malcolm – that the process is still incomplete. The Christian life is a pilgrimage, a journey to a celestial city; on that pilgrimage one cannot expect to have a full knowledge either of the road ahead or of the place to which you go. Consequently it is perfectly appropriate to have one's earlier explorations in print as well as one's later discoveries. Together they form a map of the pilgrimage so far.

A discovery I made in my conversations with him relates very closely to this, and that is that he has a minimal interest in theology or the intricacies of doctrine. This is not to say that he cannot think theologically – his discussion of the Trinity, for example, was sharply incisive and relied upon a very precise use of terms – but that he is simply not interested in the subject as an academic activity. Malcolm's attitude to theology reminds me irresistibly of his attitude to food. The Muggeridges eat well; Kitty is an excellent cook, and most of their food is home-grown or produced on local farms. There is plenty of it, it is served with grace and eaten with enthusiasm. But neither Malcolm nor Kitty are much interested in the finer issues of food production, protein content or calorific values. They simply eat and enjoy it. And Malcolm is very happy to talk about his enjoyment of God, but will not readily be drawn into abstract discussion of his essence or nature. No doubt that is why his writings have spoken so powerfully to men and women everywhere. It is not the food theorists who satisfy hunger, but those who set a generous table.

Nevertheless, Malcolm's enjoyment of God is expressed in an illuminating and often pungent way. If I were asked what he has taught me in our conversations, one answer would be that he has shown me the limitations of religious language. An odd thing to be taught, perhaps, by a self-confessed vendor of words, a man whose written output is

115

equivalent to writing the Encyclopaedia Britannica several times over (the statistic is his own; he announces it with gloomy satisfaction). But it is true. Time after time he quotes from past writers who have felt the same way: Saint Augustine, returning from his mystical vision, 'to the sound of our own speech, in which each word has a beginning and an end'; Cardinal Newman, who complained that we can speak only in allegories; Blaise Pascal, who was a brilliant scientist, the inventor of the computer, and yet remarked, 'How few things there are which can be proved . . .'

When we talked about the Holy Spirit I mentioned to Malcolm that one of the things which gave me, as an evangelical Christian, some problems in what he said was that he referred to the Holy Spirit as 'it'. This was, I explained, something which most evangelical writers would tend to regard as an error, because it implied that the Holy Spirit was not personal. 'But in what sense do you use the word "he"?' Malcolm countered. 'You can't use it in the sense that we call Jesus Christ "he", because Jesus was incarnate. He was a man, so we can use the word "he" just as we would use it of any man. But the Holy Spirit was never a man.' It was clear from Malcolm's discussion that his unwillingness to use the word 'he' to refer to the Holy Spirit was neither a devaluing of the Spirit's personhood, nor was it a downgrading of the Spirit in relation to God the Father and Jesus Christ. It was just that Malcolm felt that the word was inadequate, that there was a truth involved which words could not express. I realised how often I had slipped into a mental picture of the Holy Spirit as a kind of invisible Jesus Christ, a man I could not see. While I do not entirely agree with every detail of Malcolm's concept of the Holy Spirit, his questioning of traditional language has made me think much more deeply about the implications of the word 'Spirit'.

Another thing I have learned from Malcolm and Kitty Muggeridge is what holiness means.

'Holiness' is a word which if mentioned today in many quite ordinary social circles would raise an automatic snigger. It is used as a synonym for anaemic, joyless living; almost a denial of life itself. But even in its correct dictionary sense, the word, as Malcolm would certainly agree, is inadequate and limited. The conventional connotations have little to do with the house at Robertsbridge. There is no long-faced solemnity there. They laugh a lot. The lack of television, alcohol and meat is not asceticism or puritanism. Malcolm can be acid-tongued, and some of his victims might easily complain that they had experienced little Christian charity at his hands. But he is not prepared to sacrifice truth on the altar of charity. He cares for truth, and he trounces those who corrupt it.

Holiness is evident at Park Cottage in particular, and in general. It is evident in the miracle of the relationship between Malcolm and Kitty; their marriage is clearly the centre of their existence, and a beautiful thing for an outsider to observe. They do not talk much about marriage as a concept or an ideal. They practise it, in the way that Malcolm is attentive to Kitty's slightest need, in the way they speak to each other, in the way they look at each other. For a couple who married in the assumption that theirs was to be an 'open marriage', with each partner free to engage in any extra relationship that they fancied, their life together now is a miracle of grace.

Holiness is evident in the way that they will break off a discussion with somebody who has travelled from London to interview them, so that they can give their full attention and interest to a neighbour who has called by to say hello.

They treat people purely as people, whoever they are and whatever the business that has brought them to their home. You feel that a travelling brush-salesman calling in to ply his wares would leave somewhat shaken by the warmth of love that radiates from the Muggeridges.

And, too, holiness is evident in the general sense. There is a calm and peacefulness in their home which wraps it round, a sense of the presence of God. You enter with pleasure, and leave with regret.

Then, also, I learned from Muggeridge a great deal about the mystical implications of biblical Christianity. I knew that many people had described him as a 'mystic', meaning by that that he was in some way departing from the biblical tradition. I was wary of accepting that from the beginning; the word 'mysticism', like 'puritanism', 'socialism' and a good many other 'isms', covers a wide spectrum of meaning. I have many of the writings of Christian mystics on my shelves, and some of them, like Friedrich von Hugel, are among my best-loved Christian writers. Equally, one can see the difficulties that some mystical writers have got into by too great a dependence on their inner discoveries and too weak a dependence on the externals of the faith (the Bible and the Church, to name only two). So I was very interested in finding out what sort of a mystic Malcolm is.

He exemplifies the definition given by W. R. Inge: 'Mysticism may be defined as . . . the attempt to realise, in thought and feeling, the immanence of the temporal in the eternal, and of the eternal in the temporal.' For Malcolm, the whole of earthly life is lived in the awareness and the nearness of the reality that lies outside time; the drama (to use a favourite image) is played out with the author as audience. But it is not a flesh-hating or world-despising mysticism. I was most dramatically reminded of this when I visited him one day in October, and he suggested I join him and Kitty on one of their favourite walks in the local countryside.

It was a crisp autumn afternoon: the sky was full of small ragged clouds scudding across deep blue space. We strode up the slope of a field which I had last seen on television, when Malcolm and Kitty had strolled there with Stalin's daughter, locked in an amiable conversation while the television camera toiled after them recording it all. A bizarre contrast between the personal friendship and the public performance which is somewhat characteristic of the Muggeridges, who after two famous volumes of autobiography and innumerable public appearances by Malcolm are used to living their lives in public.

As we walked, Malcolm continued the conversation begun earlier in the house, expounding the themes of the utter folly of earthly powers and the silliness of earthly pretensions – topics familiar in his writings. But as we walked, talking of the frailty and transitoriness of this world, he kept stopping in his tracks to call out delightedly to Kitty. 'Isn't it an absolutely wonderful day? Do you not think it is lovely weather?' Anyone less gifted in words would have become boring, so often did he stop to enthuse, but he kept hauling new and fresh descriptions from an apparently inexhaustible supply, to celebrate the world's loveliness.

I found myself thinking it paradoxical that Muggeridge, who has never concealed his sense of being alien in the world and at odds with those who try to make it their proper home, should reveal himself in this way to be so shamelessly in love with it. When I reminded him of this on a later visit, he laughed. 'But you don't have to be deluded by the world to appreciate its beauty!' he remarked. I suggested that he had something in common with Thomas Traherne, whose privately-written *Centuries* have the same note of realism about the world's pretensions and glory in its wonders. 'Traherne is a very great favourite of mine,' he agreed.

And indeed, the parallel is strong.

> You never enjoy the world aright, till the Sea itself floweth in your veins, till you are clothed with the heavens, and crowned with the stars: and perceive yourself to be the sole heir of the whole world, and more than so, because men are in it who are every one sole heirs as well as you. Till you can sing and rejoice and delight in God, as misers do in gold, and Kings in sceptres, you never enjoy the world. (Traherne, *Centuries* XXIX)

For Traherne, to glory in the world in this way does not mean that one is blind to the fallenness of man.

> There is so much blindness and ingratitude and damned folly in it. The world is a mirror of infinite beauty, yet no man sees it. It is a Temple of Majesty, yet no man regards it. It is a region of Light and Peace, did not men disquiet it. It is the Paradise of God . . . (Traherne, *Centuries* XXXI)

I discussed this with Malcolm. We had been talking about death, a subject he loves to talk about, and I had quoted to him George Bernanos: 'When I die, tell them that I loved this dear world more than I can say.'

> Yes, I know the quotation. There's nothing irrational in this, you know. When I've written about dying I have always emphasised this strange fact; that on being

brought near to one's leaving this world, – without
having any illusions about it – one is still aware to a
very sharp and poignant degree of its beauties and the
things that it offers.

I looked out of his window. The sun was streaming through
the trees in the orchard, dappling the cropped lawn with
blotches of light; in the distance, the hens cackled faintly
over some quarrel or other. It was all very peaceful.

*Would you feel the same way if you lived in a city instead
of in this village?*

Oh, I think if I lived in a city I would just die. The
twentieth century town is a sort of a nightmare, and
I think people realise this.

Enjoying the world does not blind him to the fact that the
world is fallen. Nevertheless I found myself leaving him
after a visit with a heightened enjoyment of the natural
world, in much the same way as going to a concert with a
friend instead of on your own tends to increase the enjoyment you receive.

As for his Christianity, I never doubted it; it was not
one of things I came to Robertsbridge to question. The
Bible does not give us grounds to question the profession
of somebody who verbally acknowledges Christ as Lord
and lives his life as if Christ is indeed at the centre. Besides,
I had seen too many instances of Malcolm publicly defending the faith and heard too many cases of the Muggeridges'
private counselling of individuals to doubt that so far as I
was concerned, Malcolm and Kitty were Christians by any
definition I wanted to use.

My interest in Muggeridge's faith lay not in doubting it

but in wanting to know more about it – hence this book. When we talked about the process of becoming a Christian, I found myself once more rethinking my own assumptions – not questioning whether I was a Christian, but re-examining the words I was using to describe it.

If there was one area of our discussions where I substantially disagreed with Malcolm, it would be the question of whether there was a point when he became a Christian or whether for him it was a gradual growth into faith. I am fairly sure that if one knew him well and talked with him regularly over a long period, one could pinpoint a particular time in his life when he became a new creature, and before which he would not have been a Christian in any biblical sense of the notion, though Malcolm does not entirely agree with this, as can be seen in our conversations.

I have wondered sometimes when that point might have been, but I have not got very far in working out when it was. Was it at Cambridge, when he encountered living Christian faith in an everyday environment? Was it in Calcutta, at the Home for Dying Destitutes, where Mother Teresa confounded his large statements about God by simple observations ('I am sure you would understand beautifully everything if you would only "become" a little child in God's hands')? What validity does his childhood 'awareness of the infinite' have? Was his perpetual feeling, of being a 'stranger in a strange land', a sign of grace – or merely a premonition of the fall? Those long years outside the Church ringing the bell to encourage others to enter in; were they years of deprivation, when Muggeridge was prevented from joining the Body of Christ because of the failings of the visible Church – or was he just a loner with problems?

I do not know. It was a question I brought to Roberts-bridge; I took it away unanswered. But in between, I realised that it really didn't matter very much. The Bible, I realised, does not ask the question, 'When did you become a Christian?' The preoccupation of the New Testament is not what happened, or how, at some determined point in the past. The question that is asked, and is asked over and over, is: Where is your heart now? Once you were dead, writes Paul to the early Christians, but now you are alive; but he does not demand an account of the precise moment the transition took place. In any case, we are discouraged from pursuing such enquiries in respect of other people. God alone knows these things for sure; we do not. The details of exactly when and how Malcolm Muggeridge passed from death to life are known to God. It is quite possible they are not precisely known by Malcolm. And there is no biblical reason to imagine that anybody else will necessarily be able to find them out.

I think of my own experience. When did I become a Christian? Like many who were brought up in Christian homes, and many who were not, I cannot put a date on it. Was it the time when, after a particularly challenging sermon at my local Brethren assembly, I knelt (literally) at the side of my bed as a child and communicated with God? I can't even remember what it was I said, but something important was going on, else why should it have stuck in my mind these thirty years? Several years later, I was baptised by immersion. Was it then, in those shy interviews beforehand with Mr. Boulton our senior elder, that I was converted? I do not know; again, something important was happening. Years later again, in Switzerland, I woke at four in the morning, stiff and sore on a mountain top, listening to the tuneless cowbells in the distance, aware that God was in that place and that the questions I had brought there had been answered. Conversion? Perhaps. I

123

only know, with Malcolm Muggeridge, that whereas once I was blind, now I see.

As a Presbyterian discussing these matters with someone who has recently joined a Church which I could never see myself joining, there are bound to be differences between us. In different circumstances, lengthy debates might have been appropriate. We occasionally strayed into controversy, but it was unsatisfactory; there was so much to share as fellow-believers that it seemed a waste of time. These things are worth discussing, but my intention was to find out what Malcolm's Christianity meant to him in daily life, not to embark on a critique of his beliefs.

The single most important thing I have learned from him is a re-emphasis; that the fellowship of the gospel is a fellowship of ordinary human beings, drawn from all sorts of background into the unity of Christ. It has to do with truth; it has to do with how one relates to the man, Jesus Christ, who is God and who is truth. To enter that fellowship is the most straightforward thing in the world, whether one knows the time and place of it or not. To know whether that entrance has taken place, to know whether one is a Christian or not, is equally straightforward. To know whether God accepts and forgives you is something which is made possible through the words of Christ, his death and resurrection, the written word of Scripture and the ministry of the Holy Spirit. Thereby one leaves the City of Destruction, and becomes a pilgrim through this confused and wonderful world, in fellowship with others of like mind, travelling to that other City, where all our bright hopes become certainties.